Professional
Tele-Marketing Skills
The Master Guide to Selling on Phone

With emphasis on B2B & Key Accounts
…Increase Market Penetration, Save Time, Money, Energy & Efforts!

By
Gerard Assey
© Copyright 2021 by Author

Publishing Agency:
Collection Skills
19/18, Palli Arasan Street
Anna Nagar East
Chennai - 600 102

ISBN: 978-81-952564-1-9

Contents

Preface

Thank you and Congratulations on obtaining a copy of this powerful book titled: **"Professional Tele-Marketing Skills-** *The Master Guide to Selling on Phone"* which has been designed exclusively for you- to help you be better at the job and more professional.
As you will notice later, after reading the book that it has been uniquely designed, to help transform you into a Master Tele-Marketer by helping you discover the secrets that drive the world's top tele-sales professionals.
It will help you or your team create the habits and lasting changes by enabling you replace current unacceptable patterns that are costing your company sales with new ones, that will now help you achieve your sales goals faster and more consistently
And this book has been written at a time when the COVID pandemic has undoubtedly pushed organizations into rethinking ways and means to continue to operate their businesses, especially with the restrictions on safe distancing. The world over is adjusting to COVID, with social distancing orders having compelled people to find alternatives to face-to-face meetings, by working from homes or remote locations. As a result, telemarketing solutions have never been more popular than this time, as in order to conduct business without disruption, professionals and businesses have now turned more than ever before to tele-calling to stay connected with their team members and customers.

The entire book has been split into several step by step, easy and digestible modules, to help you take back and put to practice each step into a real life situation. That way these skills that you will learn will stay with you, enabling you to become more professional and successful in a sales role using the phone.
Interestingly, you will find that this entire program is suitable for anyone relatively new to selling, as well as, the more experienced ones, who wish to refresh or fine tune their existing skills, by giving it a more professional and systematic way of working, in line with today's' need for this type of consultative or relationship building approach.
Hopefully by the time you complete this entire program, it will benefit you in several ways...
Firstly, to ensure that you are equipped with the professional skills, that will not only help you in the business world, but on the personal side as well. It will provide a step by step professional approach that will enable you take your customers through, to help them deal with you in ways, as you will see later, using a consultative or relationship building approach, thus leading to a lasting relationship. This in turn will help you and the organization you work for to obtain repeat business and referrals.
You will also find that after this program, you will be able to better manage yourself as well as be able to better manage your customers-both external as well as internal!

"Professional Tele-Marketing Skills-*The Master Guide to Selling on Phone"* will provide a very structured, formatted, step by step approach guiding even a novice as well as the most experienced telesales person into professionalism that will help '**win and keep customers for life'**!

You, the reader will be able to:

- *Derive the benefits from the effectiveness of consultative selling and how different it is from the traditional sales approach*
- *Learn how to guide prospects through the buying process*
- *Proven behaviors that make you stand out as a telesales professional*
- *A thorough understanding of the attributes and activities of a professional telesales person*
- *Effectively prepare for any telesales call*
- *Make cold calls in a professional manner, right from handling gate-keepers and getting through to the right decision-makers*
- *Be able to manage your data and lists much better*
- *Build rapport and trust with a customer right during the approaching stage itself.*
- *Effectively uncover a customer's needs, problems and opportunities and be able to demonstrate how your product features can help a customer meet a need/solve a problem (proving value).*
- *Overcome objections, cope with turn-downs, rejection or call reluctance*
- *Be able to recommend an appropriate solution (recommending) and close business deals effectively after showing a customer how specific business objectives can be met and benefit by using your recommended product or service (closing)*
- *Effectively and professionally sell to B2B/ Key Accounts using a structured approach*
- *Implement the entire consultative selling process into your daily work*
- *And…most importantly, in every chapter or topic that is covered, there are several exercises for you to work on and put the new skills to immediate use.*

After reading the book, you will be able to gain a full understanding of both the buying and selling processes, including the importance of being well organized. And over the period, you would have worked through the six step process of a structured telesales call, practicing and mastering the skills at each stage, so that your selling skills are developed and reinforced

With no gimmicks, no jargon, just emphasis on relationship building, I believe that this is a well structured course on 100% building value and long lasting partnerships with your customer!

Before you move forward on this exciting journey that I am about to take you through, I would recommend that you have a note pad and pen to make notes of important points along with completing the exercises provided, that you can start using immediately.

So are you ready to embark on this exciting journey with me? Take your time, sit back and enjoy these learning's!

How to get the most out of this book

This book was written to help following categories of people:
- People interested in entering into the telemarketing field
- Current telemarketers and telesales professionals looking to take their telephone sales skills to the next dimension and generate even greater results
- Traditional salespeople looking to now use the telephone as a powerful sales tool enabling them save time, resources, and money (especially during a pandemic).
- Sales managers or call center supervisors who work with or manage teams of telemarketers.
- Business owners looking to expand their business and reach a larger customer base

So whether you are new to telemarketing or a seasoned professional looking to improve your skills, this book will help take you step by step through many of the challenges faced by most telemarketers by providing you a well structured approach.

And here are some ways to help you get the best out of this book:
1. Make a commitment to dedicate a fixed amount of time each day/week: The results will depend on the time and efforts you put in to follow on the self-paced process that this book will take you through
1) Decide what you want to get out of this book- the objective and how you intend doing this?
2) You must decide initially to get out of your comfort zone if you are to experience success from this.
   Remember: *'If you continue to do what you've always done, you will continue to get what you've always got!'* If you are looking at different (better) results, you must then look at doing different things and different ways!
3) The road to success is already walked and laid out for you. Someone has already been through the *'School of Hard Knocks'*! You don't have to waste time re-inventing the wheel.
4) Put the ideas to immediate practice-Apply the ideas to your selling situation. No idea or concept is worth anything, if it cannot be applied to real situations. So applying these principles by putting them to immediate practice is the KEY! The book will help you translate the concepts into your own specific situations right away.
5) Work on expanding your knowledge: Do additional reading/ listening/ watching videos/ CD's …whatever that can help you stay ahead!
6) Keep a record of your new learning's/ experience in using them and your accomplishments. This is YOUR own workbook…Go ahead scribble, make notes. The words you read are really nothing. It's what you work on as you go along and put to practice is what really counts. The tools, exercises and checklists are designed to help you be more organized and sell more successfully.

7) Learn to share with others how these ideas have helped you: That way these new skills and techniques help get embedded into your system.
8) Finally, learn to have fun with every progressive step.
9) Now Enough of Theory! Let's just start by putting it into Practice!

The Sales Profession! Why it is the most fascinating, YET most hated profession?

For many of you that have decided to make Sales as your career and for those already in it for a number of years, you would have already begun to realize that this is one of the most fascinating, rewarding and the fastest 'climb-up-the-ladder' professions. In fact the 'majority' of Chief Executives you see today that head organizations have mostly moved up from the sales rung.

Yet sadly, it is also the most hated profession worldwide. For many years I was inhibited about getting into the sales profession for various reasons, and always opted for a 'behind the scenes job'. I had always perceived a salesperson to be untrustworthy, that used high-pressure tactics. How sad that a group consisting of a good percentage of the working public is thought to be so! And I believe, I could have lost out on a lot because of that and it was only much later in life, after getting into it, (by chance, not choice), did I realize what a fascinating profession it is to be in and how much of a contribution a sales person makes to others- his customers, his family, his company, the industry, the economy...it can go on, as you will see soon.

Why is Selling such a Great Profession?
Selling is filled with great opportunities! Unfortunately, the profession is tarnished, with 9/10 using a very unprofessional approach. And we (even you and I are customers!) remember only the bad.

However, it is said that the average sales person keeps more than 30 people employed! It is also the oldest and largest income group in the world (Why oldest? The very first humans- Eve sold the idea to Adam of having the Apple in the Garden of Eden!)

It is the only field where there is:
-No real need for qualifications (If you have it helps further!)
-Age is no asset or liability
-Men/ women regardless of previous experience or employment are motivated to get in.
-A sense of pride: "I am a sales person"
-Impressive income- you write your own pay check-unlimited
-Fastest growth-unlimited opportunities
-Flexibility
-Independence
-Constant recognition
-People-networking
-Exposure
-Knowledge-self improvement/ updating of knowledge
-You have personal security- a future: You may lose tangible wealth, but can regain all with proper attitude. You can always get back into this profession, even after few years of being out!
-Can be a good influence to others to improve themselves.

-Fun along the way

Just think of it: Our country and some of the other world powers wouldn't be great economies if it were not for some of the great sales people that make great sales every day! How about the book that you hold in your hands? Ever wondered how it got so far? It got there because thousands of sales people sold something.

Let us start from the scratch and see this book as an example!
In order for this book to exist, a sales person first had to sell seeds and fertilizers to a farmer. Then a sales person had to sell trees to a paper mill. For the trees to be harvested and cut down, someone had to sell logging equipment to a logging contractor. In order to get the logs to the paper mill, someone had to sell a special lorry or truck to transport them.
For a paper mill to exist, it takes an investment of several millions. Somebody had to sell the banks on the idea that this would be a good investment. Research indicates that for a paper mill to be built it takes about several sales calls, several proposals, and several sales closed, not forgetting a good number of sales cancelled too.
After the paper is manufactured, somebody had to sell the paper for this book to the printer. For this book to be printed, somebody had to sell the printer a printing press, someone a binding machine, someone a trimmer, someone a packing machine etc. Don't forget the design that went into this book and the equipment required for that. The printing company would not be in business, if it were not for its sales team calling on publishing houses. A book like this would not exist if it were not for the sales efforts of people like YOU- the sales team!

Yes, nothing happens unless somebody sells something!!

Selling is a wonderful profession. Just think of some of the salespeople who were involved in selling the machinery for the paper mill or the printing equipment. Some of them could have made enough and more to buy a resort or even an island. Yes, great things happen when someone sells something and does it well.
Now think of the budgets to run huge sales forces, the laptops, telephone lines, internet connections, the software, presentation equipment, air tickets, hotel stays, conference calls, meetings, incentives and sales leads to call on new prospects. Yes only in this profession can you create wealth and redistribute wealth.
The best part is that selling is one of the best performing arts. The best actors make their art disappear...the same is true with great sales people. They don't focus on selling, because people hate being sold by pushy sales people. Customers on the contrary love to buy from great sales people.
Great Sales people don't sell- they just help people get want they want...as this book does. Yes, I believe with all my heart that it will help you get what you want too!

As we've just seen-Everything starts with a Sale! Surveys reveal that 74 to 84% of all revenue is generated from a Sales Persons Activity.

So why then- when there is much good about this profession, why is it the MOST HATED Profession?
You don't have to look far- If you see the gates of some of the buildings (particularly in Asian Countries), you will find signs put up: 'SALESMEN NOT ALLOWED'. And at the side of these, you will also find another sign that goes like this: 'DOGS NOT ALLOWED'. Isn't this sad? And with tele-calling it is even worse as people think it is an intrusion… Sadly, such a powerful profession that has been looked down and literally 'hated' by the general public! I have for a major part of my career been in this profession and it is really depressing seeing these signs.
The question now is: Why do most people generally hate or avoid sales people? Why is this profession so tarnished?
In a recent survey, customers cited 80 various reasons why they hated Sales People. We will not be getting into all the 80 reasons, but let us just look at the top 7 reasons: Ranking no.1 was 'not listening' followed by 'talking too much' I believe these two go hand in hand. How much better it would be if the sales person just spent more time listening and the amount of information he or she would be able to gather by doing so. Next on the list was a lack of product, market or industry knowledge, which has an effect on one's credibility to a great extent, leading to distrust. Studies reveal that Trust is the bond or cement to a lasting relationship.
Fourth on the list is a lack of Follow-up. In other words, promises and commitments never kept, or false promises provided, which again leads to effecting credibility and eventually creating distrust.
The 5th top reason is one of the attributes that I see very often from sales people who would do whatever it takes to get that order or business, and this comes from an inner lack of confidence or belief in oneself, company, product or service, coupled with the lack of overall knowledge. This leads to the sales person having to now bluff his way, to get the sale….and again leading to effecting the credibility and trust between the buyer and seller.
One of the main reasons why a sale is lost is that the sales person failed to take time in understanding the needs of the customer- which is now our 6th reason of why customers hate sales people. We will cover a lot on this in a later chapter.
Finally, the 7th top reason why customers hate salesmen is that the salesperson cannot or refuses to take a 'no' for an answer. We must realize that not everyone out there can be your customer or that the 'would have been customer 'did not see value in your products or service. This is because the customer was pushed with the features of the service, instead of the sales person explaining the benefits of what the product or service would do for the customer and the ultimate benefit or value he would gain if he did so! We'll cover more on this too in a separate chapter later.
And as I mentioned earlier, with tele-calling it is even worse- with tele-callers calling at odd hours, not revealing their true identity/ caller ID, calls from the same few companies literally dozens of times for a day trying to sell stuff that one may never need- thinking that if they bug someone enough, they'll buy from them! And lots more 'put-offs'!
But remember, finally, that the profession that you are in is **an honorable profession** and the only way we can stand out and make a difference is to stay professional, by avoiding these annoying traits- and that is what this book will help you do.

<u>**EXERCISE**</u>
Ask yourself (or maybe do it with someone who could provide you with honest feedback) and list down all the possible traits that you could sometimes be exhibiting unknowingly that can put customers off!

(Some examples to help you: *calling at odd hours, wrong or false commitments, pressurizing, unwilling to give customer a chance to talk- not listening, standard or canned script for every customer, a monotonous non enthusiastic tone in voice, rattling off the features of your products without understanding customers need…*)

Note: After you have your list, make an Action plan with a time frame on eliminating these annoying traits)

The Tele-sales Profession and what the telephone can help you do

Telemarketing is the effective use of the telephone as a marketing tool in a structured manner to help a business achieve its objectives and if executed well and professionally, can be a truly successful, profitable and mutually beneficial channel of communication and sales between you and your customer.

It gives you an invaluable opportunity to communicate highly relevant and personalized offers to your customer in a timely and sensitive manner.

Here are some key advantages of Tele-Marketing: The Benefits of Selling on Phone!

- Very Economical-Saves travel time, parking, chatting, waiting time and fuel costs. it is very much inexpensive compared to having a sales representative out on field
- It is Personal -More personal than a letter. You can speak to the person direct. It is highly interactive
- Management of Anxiety-Expressions are concealed, negative facial expressions cannot be seen.
- Excellent and Time-saving way to screen lists-otherwise too time consuming and costly. It can reach a wide geographical area and target more people compared to a sales person calling on those individuals in person.
- It is Flexible- It can be used from any location as and when a person wishes.
- Productivity Enhanced-More calls, coverage and reach over phone in shortest span of time-Deeper penetration
- Direct touch with Decision Makers-Saves chances of postponement and middlemen. You can deal with queries and objections directly and immediately
- Prospects obtain Immediate Information-No delays!
- Avoids Prejudices-Prospects may not like us, but on phone all that is hidden (too young, old, trendy, shabby, etc?)
- Better Negotiations-We aren't giving ourselves and our positions away because of eye contact and body language
- No Delays on Decision- Both (customer and caller) are forced to get to the point-Saves time.
- No Closing Tensions-In person to person selling there is always that tension on both parties, when finalizing a decision-On phone it's much simpler and quicker.
- It is Controllable and Measurable- you can evaluate the results of your calls, control campaigns and monitor effectiveness.
- Social Distancing Maintained: At times such as the COVID pandemic, with social distancing being the norm, the telephone is one of the most handy instruments, not just for the sales profession but any and everyone

As can be seen from above the advantages of selling on phone are numerous, but if the call is mishandled though, it can destroy your organization's reputation and you lose valuable sales, credibility and image in one shot. So it pays to get it right.

So what are some of the disadvantages of using the telephone as a sales tool?
- You can't see the other person on phone: This can cause problems in the communication process. On the telephone, the body language aspect of communication is missing, and with this vital visual element missing, you the telemarketer would need to work harder to communicate the right image and impression. The only impression the customer, or prospect, can have of you is through your voice and attitude. Therefore, it is vital that you use your voice in the most powerful and constructive way because the prospect will make an initial judgment about you and your organization based on how you sound. People will base their judgments on what you say, or rather what they think you say and how you say it!
- You could be intruding or interrupting: The telephone is intrusive, as you may never know- you could be calling at an inconvenient time.
- The prospect may not be paying full attention: they could be doing other things whilst talking on the telephone. Because the prospect or customer can't see you, you and /or the prospect could be tempted to do other things whilst on the phone, and thus not being fully involved or listening carefully.
- More likely to jump to wrong conclusions: This is because they hear what they want to hear or could also misinterpret your tone of voice.
- Difficult to communicate accurate information: Because people remember more of what they see than hear.
- May have to pass through several 'gatekeepers' before you get to the right person
- And…Can be cut off at any time (at the most crucial part of a conversation).

The Ocean of Opportunities with Telemarketing!
Telemarketing provides a wide range of business opportunities and can be divided into two key categories:
Inbound Calls and Outbound Calls
Inbound Calls would mean receiving calls from your customers, or enquiries from prospects
Examples of Inbound Calls: Enquiries or order calls can come as a result of an advertisement placed in a newspaper, magazine, or on television or from a website with a free phone number or a low cost call number listed on it. This enables customers to call the provider to obtain advice or more information.

Outbound Calls would mean making calls to your customers and prospects to sell something and can be for many of the following reasons:
- Direct selling- retail and commercial
- Seasonal product selling

- Special promotions
- Setting appointments for field sales force/ Backing up field sales force
- Reactivating dormant accounts
- Opening new sales territories /developing prospect lists
- Cleaning prospect lists
- Database building
- Lead generation
- Qualifying/ filtering prospects
- Generating new leads
- Collecting overdue accounts
- Account handling
- Market research
- Positioning and pricing products
- Refining engineering values or product development/ application
- Fine-tuning marketing strategies
- Learning about competition
- Maintaining customer/shareholder relations
- Overcoming negative publicity
- Explaining unusual or new developments (name change, mergers or take-over, sales of company, etc.)
- Order-taking
- Solving service and parts issues
- Offering exceptional customer service.
- Identifying problems customers have and fixing them.
- Dealing with customer complaints, and then transforming them into happy customers with up-sell potential.
- Cross-selling/upgrading/ selling products/services to existing customers
- Renewing subscriptions
- Updating records (changes of addresses/ phone numbers/ email ids)
- Supplying information to queries
- Taking reservations (seminars and conferences, entertainment etc)
- Tracking advertising/promotion/publicity

Key Attributes and Characteristics of a Professional Tele-Marketer

We now know what customers hate about salespeople. Before we go any further, let us now look at what can create satisfied customers. With this understanding I am just trying to build a platform as to what would be required if we are to stand out as Professionals!

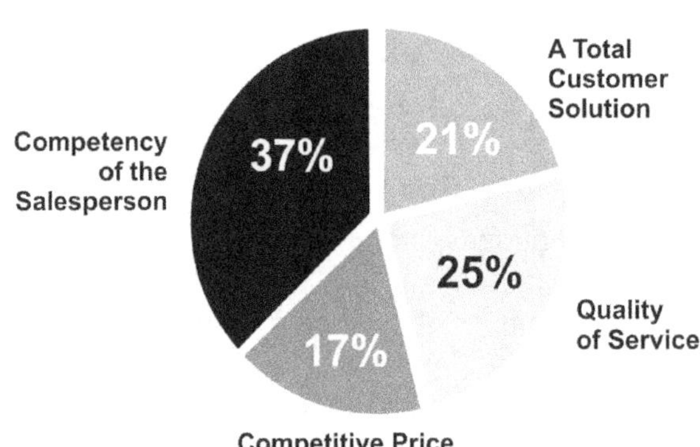

According to another survey as you will see in the illustration, 37% has to do with the 'competency of the sales person', followed by 25% on the 'quality of product or service' provided. This was followed by 21% on the 'total solution' provided by the sales person or the right solution that matched the customers need and finally 17% had to do with a 'competitive rate or price'.

Now let us look at what is in your control as a sales person.
Is the competence of the sales person in your control….certainly a big YES!
Is the quality of service in your control….A big YES again!
A total customer solution…? Off course, without a doubt a big YES again.
And finally a competitive pricing…? Even if we are to say that this area lay with management or another department, you have a good 83% of what can create satisfied

customers in your very control, so we as Sales People have no excuse in blaming anyone else when it comes to the dissatisfaction of customers.

We've just seen what creates satisfied customers….now taking this a little deeper on what the client specifically requires from your company that you represent, we can see that there are 4 vital areas:

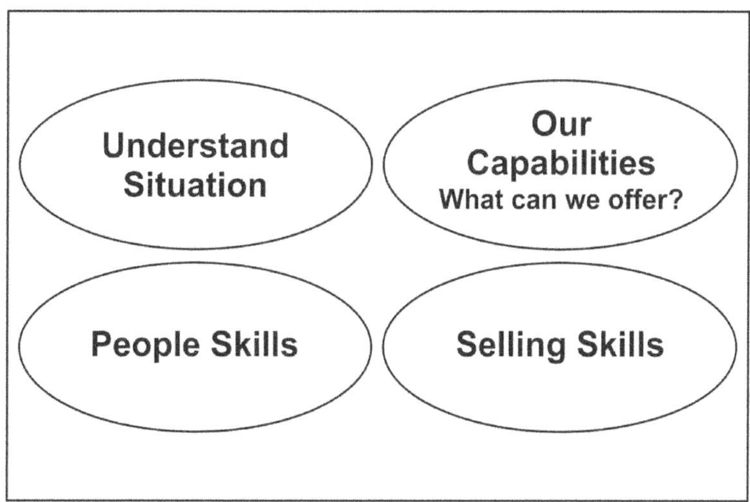

First and foremost is that:
Are we able to understand the situation of the customer, his specific needs, problems or pain areas? Are we more interested in helping him rather than just chasing for an order!
Second: would be on what have we got to offer that best matches that need that we've identified…in other words our capabilities. Have we been able to prove value of it?
How are you as a sales person, effectively going to use your skills to help him to buy; because people hate to be sold, they love to buy! In other words human beings love to own a decision for a good purchase they've made. This would be the Selling Skills part!
You are not pushing the customer, but you and the customer are working together as partners in taking a decision that can help the customer.
Finally, is the People Skills- meaning how effectively are you going to build a rapport and a long term relationship that can be a win-win situation for both the customer and your company. How courteous and friendly are you and your organization- especially when the customer does have a problem. Would your company be there when needed most?

We've just seen broadly what the client requires from you and your company. Now let us see what YOU as the salesperson will need to specifically have in order for you to achieve this objective.

While every business requires CASH to survive and succeed, every Professional Sales Person also requires something in them in order to succeed, which I believe is more valuable than that CASH. This is 'K.A.S.H.' because only when you have this K.A.S.H. in you, you will be more successful in bringing in the CASH for you and your company.

So what is this K.A.S.H.?
Knowledge
Attitude
Skills
Habits

Knowledge is all about your Company, the Products or Services that you offer, the Market and Industry that you operate in, together with knowing who are the other players or your competition that are in this industry. It also involves knowing where you stand against them-your strengths and areas that your competition has an advantage over you, along with being thorough on the rates, polices and regulations in your industry and market.

How effectively are you able to transfer this knowledge to your customers on phone to enable them to deal or decide upon you as a service provider is a skill and the major part of this book is all about that.

Now there are various types of skill sets that people possess:
Eg; Selling Skills (the book in your hand incidentally is all about this),
Some other examples for Skills are:
Time Management
Team Working
Presentation Skills
Writing Skills-Ability to present ideas in writing
Effective Communication
Negotiation Skills

Now having Knowledge and Skills alone is not enough. There are many sales people that have a great bank of knowledge along with the necessary skills, but yet have been total failures. Reason being, they had a lousy attitude or very poor habits that killed a potential sale or the potential in them; that ultimately affected theirs and their organizations credibility

What you are seeing on the pie chart is the mental make-up of a Professional Sales Person.

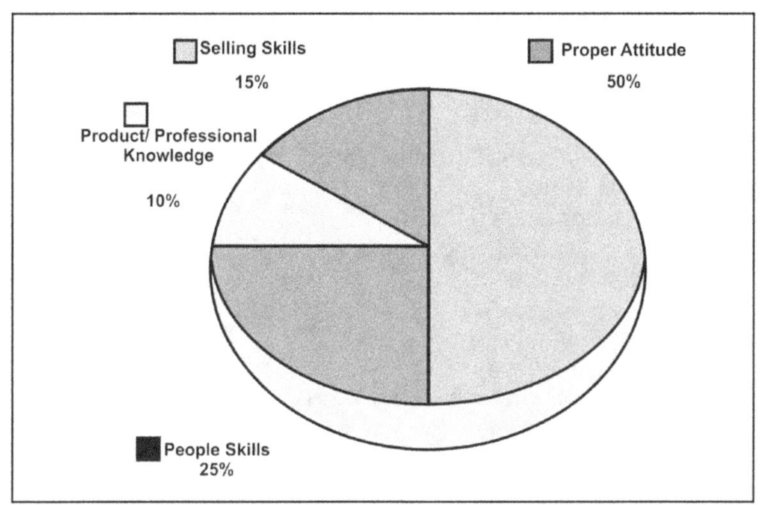

As you will see, 50% has to do with the Attitude, followed by 25% on People Skills. In other words, if you don't have the required knowledge or skills to sell, as you can see, you will be able to still succeed with the right attitude and people skills, because those two account for 75%. Now don't get me wrong, I am not saying that you should not work on your knowledge and skills…Absolutely no!

What I am saying is that given that you have the right attitude coupled with the right people skills, knowledge and selling skills, you don't have to guess where your sales would be!

For a telemarketer, a potential customer's perception of any company is based on how you as the telemarketer handles the initial moment of contact. If those of us in business were to ask all our customers how they first made contact with us it is highly likely that more than 80% did so by telephone. With most of the business deals half completed on the phone before a face to face contact is made, it is therefore all the more crucial for businesses to ensure that their teams are trained properly, as the problem with telephones is that people can't be impressed by the size of your office, the smile on your face, or the clothes you're wearing. They have only two things to go by- your **Attitude** and your **Voice**. People who call your office only once will base 90 percent of what they think of your company on that one call.

Let us look at this a little differently….Assuming you have the right attitude and people skills, which together comprise of 75% but lack the required knowledge and skills, well then, to me with the right attitude you can easily learn them. In any case Knowledge and Selling Skills are teachable, but not Attitude!

Attitude is the outlook or perception towards a given situation, and for a sales person this is crucial and foundational! Attitude is made up from our upbringing, environment, exposure etc. It would therefore be extremely difficult or it would take a long time to undo a wrong attitude that has gone in all these years. And for a Sales Person this is very important- as customers remember the wrong or negative attitude longer. You are the only thing the customer sometimes sees of your company- and this is the impression formed of your entire company- good or bad! It a takes a long time to undo this negative feeling about your company in the mind of the customer.

At this stage it is important to realize that there are **3 A's** of **Business life**:
Ability, Ambition and Attitude.
Ability establishes *'what'* someone does
Ambition determines *'how much'* he does
Attitude *'guarantees how'* he does it!

Ability will bring one a pay cheque
Ambition will get him a raise
Attitude alone will lead to success in everything!

Attitude is actually the 'YOU on the job. When ability and ambition in two people are about equal, how does the boss select one over the other for promotion? Here is where Attitude is the deciding factor. Attitude reflects a little plus- that something extra is given willingly though not required.
If you look at the word A-T-T-I-T-U-D-E itself, is it a mere coincidence that "I" comes first and "U" later? If this has any significance, then in trying to understand the attitudes of people, we should first examine ourselves in relation to other people!
Because Attitude is so very important, this is why it is so crucial to fill our minds with the right positive thoughts because our thoughts work into decisions that form our actions and this continued action leads to a habit, which eventually makes up our attitude. Your habits today will become your attitude in the days to come. That's why it is important to check our habits as well. As an example: The habit of late-coming, if not nipped in the early stages can lead it to becoming an attitude, with everything that you undertake being late or delayed!
Here are some examples of positive or right attitude:
Belief
Commitment
Desire
Ability to fail
Persistent goals
Self-Motivation
Enthusiasm
Purpose
Self-discipline
Confidence
Creativity
Empathy
Go the extra mile
Self-improvement
Time organization
…and most of all the *PASSION!*

Successful Sales People…
-Understand themselves and how their behavior affects their customers
-Have a positive attitude, which reflects in dedication to getting it right the first time, and
  commitment to help colleagues to help their customers
-Know how to adapt their behavior to meet the differing needs of the situation
-A willingness to take responsibility
-Have the confidence to stay calm under pressure

Steps to change your Attitude …
-Become aware of your negative attitude towards yourself, other people and situations
 and alter your thinking
-Think for yourself and become more constructive
-Keep an open mind

Remember: Changes are always: M.A.D.E…!!!
Developing Sales Attitudes is not something that happens to you-it is something you
make happen…and like any change, it is not easy!
M- Mental Pictures: Visualize who you are, what you want, how will you conduct and
carry yourself on phone
A- Affirmations: Add a new self-image by talking positively
D- Daily Successes: Build confidence everyday by looking at your positives rather than
negatives
E- Environmental Influences: Surround yourself with positive influencers, read positive
stuff, listen and watch positive information etc

***You are what you think! To change any habits, you must first change any
thoughts, feelings and values!***

Changing Bad Habits into Good Ones!
STEP # 1: List your bad habits
STEP # 2: What were the original causes?
STEP # 3: What are the supporting causes?
STEP # 4: Determine a positive habit to replace the bad one.
STEP # 5: Think about the good habit, its benefits and results.
STEP # 6: Take action to develop this habit.
STEP # 7: Daily act upon this habit for reinforcement.
STEP # 8: Reward yourself by noting one of the benefits from your good habit

EXERCISE
1. List some of the Key **Attitudes, Skills** and **Habits** that you possess?
2. List some of the **Attitudes, Skills** and **Habits** that you lack or are weak in and
   need to work on?
3. By 'when' and 'what' will you do specifically, to improve or change the negatives
   to positives?
4. Action Plan

Your Professional Image:
Sell yourself before you sell anything else!

A very important part that we would be touching on now is that of how we communicate or the impressions we create even before we could open our mouths.
In a study carried out that I am about to share with you now, you will notice that people place more emphasis on what they SEE rather than on what they HEAR.
So this only tells us that we need to be very careful with our body language and what we are projecting.
According to studies carried out, Communication takes place in 3 forms:
Your Words
Your Tone and
Your Body Language.
Where 55% has to do with your BODY LANGUAGE or what others SEE
7 % has to do with WHAT you say or your words
Whilst 38% has to do with HOW those words are said, which is your Tone or voice modulation

With people going by what they SEE first rather than what they HEAR, it makes it very important for us to therefore project the RIGHT image upfront. That's the impression that has been formed-good or bad! If it is good, then very good for you, but if it is bad, then so sad! Because…now you have double work to undo the wrong impression that has already gone into the mind and to now fill it with the right impression.
They say 90% of lasting impressions are created in the first 90 seconds. That can be really dangerous, but surprisingly that is true! So we have to be very careful, with what are we projecting as soon as someone sees us, because that's what they will remember. (Now you could be wondering why are we covering on body language, when the customer will not be seeing us…but hold on till the end of this chapter to know how this impacts your call!)
It is also a reason why we tend to remember a song seen on a television set better than when heard through a radio. The same logic applies at a job interview with your resume and the presentation of it! Then at the interview-the interviewer has made up his mind to a great extent as you walk in, even before you have opened your mouth. Your bio-profile or the interview process is only a confirmation of the decision already made in the mind of the interviewer.
Why is Tone next important after Body Language? Simply because you can say a same sentence with a different tone and that can change the entire meaning
Eg; *"Sarah come here"* is a simple sentence. But depending on the right tone this one sentence could turn out as an 'order 'or a 'request'.
Another stronger example: *"Hang him not let him go"*…could be death or life depending on how it is said. Example: *'Hang him, not let him go'!* Or *'Hang him not, let him go'!*

Now, if it is face to face, we may be able to save the situation, but when on the phone with the other person not able to see you, it could lead to miscommunication if the right tone is not used.

Sp here are a few aspects of voice quality that you can work on to improve your vocal image!

- Pitch/Tone: Too high, too low, ruff or irritating to the ear becomes noticeable and distracting. Record your voice, listen, work on improving vocal skills, and assess progress.
- Accent: Minimize your own accent and pick up the customer's speaking style, being clear and easily understood.
- Volume: Being too loud or too soft is a habit one can change. Ask how you sound.
- Inflection: One can impose their personal interpretation upon words by effective inflection. Use a natural inflection to maintain interest-Avoid monotone.
- Enthusiasm: Communicates a personal involvement in the conversation. Having a smile will enable this together with enabling you sound friendlier.
- Conveying emotions: Use your voice to convey confidence, enthusiasm, joy, friendliness, concern, or any other emotion.
- Sincerity: You must believe in what you are doing. Communicate your belief in yourself, company and product.
- Vocabulary: The right choice of words you use to communicate
- Pacing: It's the rate and rhythm of a speech pattern. Talk the same pace as that of your customer. Studies reveal that by simply 'mirroring' or 'echoing' a customer's pacing can increase the customers understanding of what is said.
- Pronunciation: Your ability to use the language correctly

As seen earlier, with people going by what they SEE first rather than what they HEAR, it makes it so very important for you to therefore project the RIGHT image upfront. It basically involves Selling Yourself first!

Before a Customer buys anything or decides to do business with you or the company that you represent, he needs to first be sold on you because you are what he sees about your company to him. Your company could have a several floor building, with several offices all across the globe. But to the customer what he sees in you, (through this call) is the impression he has formed of your company! Because…90% of lasting impressions are created in the first 90 seconds

Importance of maintaining a good posture when on the phone

If you slouch when you make a call, the prospect will actually be able to hear it in your voice. As well as impacting on the confidence and energy of the call, it can affect the tone of your voice. So before picking up the phone to call a prospect, telemarketers should ensure that their posture is right. Take a minute to ensure you are sitting up straight and have your shoulders back. This will instantly make you feel more energetic, more confident and more focused when you speak to the prospect.

Have all the data/ documentation for the call ready at hand. It is all about what the customer 'sees' about you as his first impression that enables him move forward.

Use the gestures as if talking to someone physically in front of you. These gestures lead to facial expression and facial expressions affect the voice and the way the voice says the words. Try it!

<u>EXERCISE</u>
What areas of your communication would you need to work on, in order to create the right positive impressions: (Your words, your tone, your body language?). Develop your own checklist now to suit your specific organization, country and need.

Why your Self-Esteem matters!
How to build a high self esteem

Confidence versus Self-Esteem
A lot has been said and published with a great debate on the subject of 'Confidence'.
A lot of Sales people want to be more confident, without knowing the actual meaning of it.
A few points to note about confidence is that; it is 'External' and it is 'Temporary'. When I say external- I mean that in most times it is <u>not</u> in your control- somebody else is most of the time controlling it. When I say it is temporary I believe that for a day our confidence levels fluctuate several times depending on situations, circumstances, the people and environment we are in. That is why we do not recommend that sales people aim at only confidence.
Here is an example of what I mean:
You come into the office in the morning in a good mood-upbeat and all excited with a set of appointments you have for the day. However, your boss calls you into his cabin and pulls you up for a complaint that has come in from a top customer. What happens to your confidence level…One that was upbeat, is now down depending on how hard he came upon you!
Later, that same evening, you have bagged a huge order from another customer and that same boss now praises you as one of his best performers. What happens now? You are on top of the world, all up beat and charged up again.
As you can see in a single day your confidence levels can vary and fluctuate, which means they are temporary. Most times it is the effect or impact of others that have changed that feeling. It is like someone having a remote control on your life and your moods that can change or impact it every now and then.
A better, permanent solution to this is for you as a sales person to work on having a High Self Esteem. First let us look at what is Self Esteem?
Simply put…It is how much you value or respect yourself! The more you value or respect yourself, then, when you do face such situations like the example we've just seen, you are able to stay above- your value if it is 100, stays 100 and does not change! You now know that your boss has pulled you up for something wrong that you had done- you do not take it personally and that does not change your value- your value still remains 100.

Building your Self Esteem
Say out loud:
"I am the Most Valuable Person at work".
"I am the Most Valuable Person at my work". (Repeat it)

It's true. You are the most valuable person. No one else can quite fill your shoes. No one else can be you. You bring your unique being to work every day. You bring with you

your talents, your abilities, your knowledge, your skills, your personality, or just your plain know-how. You may not be using all of your abilities just yet. You may not be using them to the fullest. You may not even recognize how valuable a person you are. Healthy Self Esteem, not narcissistic, self-indulgent, or arrogance means to appreciate the value of you as a unique human being with your own special talents and abilities. The word "esteem" in Latin, means, *"to value highly"*
It would be impossible to value another person without first feeling valuable for yourself. When you place value on your own work and efforts, you can begin to find value in the work of others.

The Self-Image: Highway to Success
Have you ever said to yourself the following?
'I can't imagine myself being successful'
'I would like to, but I don't have enough experience or the right education'
'My voice is not good enough as a telemarketer
'I can't get ahead because I'm too short, overweight, not good looking; my parents are poor, etc'.
The truth is most people talk themselves into failure and dejection. The result is the Fear of Trying!
Most of us know of or have read about common, everyday people who have become uncommonly productive and successful in their work and careers; individuals who have overcome enormous outer obstacles and inner roadblocks to become great.
Yet many people can't imagine doing such things themselves. They say, *"Yes, he could do it or she's doing it, but I can't because of*_______________*".*
They develop the habit of failure. And it takes two forms:
Failure Reinforcement-the habit of looking back at past problems
Failure Forecasting-the habit of imagining the worst in the future

Because they lack sufficient self-esteem to believe in the validity of their dreams and visions, they don't prepare for their achievement, and therefore are going down a dead-end street. No wonder so many people feel trapped. Failure becomes set in their self-images.
Never put yourself down- the workplace is full of put-downs- Don't do it yourself!

Self Esteem Takes Practice
Believe in yourself, no matter how long it takes or how tough it may seem at times. There was once a college professor whose wife had a hearing deficiency. In trying to invent a device to enhance her hearing, he created something more complex that he thought might be useful to the public. He traveled throughout the New England states trying to find venture capital to take his idea into production. But businessmen everywhere laughed at him. *"Ideas are a dime a dozen."* They said: *"The project is doomed to failure."* Thank goodness, Alexander Graham Bell had the self-esteem to hang in there even when his only reward was his belief in himself.
Often we put imaginary barriers in our paths when no such barriers actually exist. In the 1940s, the greatest physicist and aeronautical engineers believed that the sound barriers could not be broken- that everyone or anything would be shattered when it

approached the speed of sound. One lone pilot, Chuck Yeager, didn't believe it. He didn't think there was such a thing as sound "barrier". And indeed, he flew right through it.

Your Formula for Building a High Self-Esteem

How much you like yourself is the core energy force that determines your personality. All top performers have a program or formula for building self-esteem.

Steps You Can Take To Feel Better:
1. Action precedes feeling. Act your way into feeling something. Action triggers emotion. The role of pretending- act happy!
2. Set clear goals, so you can feel like a winner. Establish a VICTORY LIST for all your accomplishments. Set income goals (the WHAT) and personal goals (the WHY)
3. Accept 100% responsibility. "IF IT'S TO BE, IT'S UP TO ME." Or "IF IT'S ALL FOR ME, IT'S UP TO ME". No excuses, no blaming.
4. Commit yourself to excellence. LEARN TO BE THE BEST in whatever you do. Say to yourself: *'I'M THE BEST (and) I LOVE MY WORK'*
5. Mental Rehearsal: Visualize the outcomes you desire, especially before you go to sleep at night. See yourself as strong, confident and relaxed, and see your customers responding positively.
6. Get yourself a small note pad. Every night write down at least 3 positive things you did for that day- (it could be as small as even helping a person cross the road). Forget the negatives. Most times we go to bed filling our minds with all the negatives that occurred during the day. Just reverse it now. Look at only the positives. At the end of the year, you would have over one thousand positive things about you. Do you need anything else then to tell you?
7. Believe in yourself-FAITH! Believe in yourself, your company and your products.
8. INTEGRITY AND HONESTY. They are at the root of success in sales. Never expect to be successful without being willing to pay the price. Never expect the rewards without working. Don't look for shortcuts.
9. Have confident expectations. Look for the good in every situation. Expect the best.
10. Practice the Law of Increasing Returns-the more your give thanks, the more you will have thanks for.

Key Activities of a Professional Tele-Marketer (Effectively Managing your Day and Activities)

Every Sales Person, I believe has only **4 Key Activities** for a day irrespective of whatever you sell, and all what you do…it could be a 100 different things, but they broadly can be classified or covered under these 4 key headings:

Planning
Prospecting
Selling
Administration

If you had to rate these 4 activities in an order of importance- what do you think would rank as number 1, 2, 3 and 4 respectively? Have a try before you see the recommended answer that follows!

The most important activities for any Sales Person, and to put across a little stronger-is what he or she is paid to do- **Prospecting** and **Selling**. If you are spending anything lesser than 75% on these 2 areas then you would need to look at revamping your working schedule. These 2 Activities are the only ones that account for being revenue generators. The other 2 are only support functions.

Planning is the scheduling of your activities- long, medium and short term, while also including your meetings with bosses, other departments etc.
Some examples of Planning are:
Planning the next day/ week's calendar
Working on an annual or monthly sales plan
Planning the day's calls
Meeting with manager to discuss targets and results
Researching potential customers
Analysing the existing client base

Administration is the time you spend on the preparation of your reports, documentation, market feedback etc.
Some examples are:
Preparing reports
Updating customer records/ CRM
Preparing bills if any
Attending training courses

Prospecting involves time spent in sourcing new potential opportunities on phone and the bulk of your time should go here, because this is your insurance to future business. This is like a pipeline to continuous business.
Some examples are:
Tele-calling potential customers
Requesting for referrals

Cold canvassing

Selling is the actual time you spend on phone with a customer to gain business or for a business opportunity
Some examples are:
Fixing Appointments
Fact finding to uncover needs
Presentation in front of customers
Follow up for a decision
Negotiating terms and conditions
Unfortunately, many sales people fall into what is called the *'Activity Trap',* where they measure their effectiveness by how *hard* they work, rather than by how *smart* they work.

A good time to schedule your Planning and Administration Activities would be during the non peak business hours or when your customers are not usually available, as the peak of business hours should be for Prospecting and Selling, when you should be there on phone with the customer. If you are not, remember, your competition will be there!

Now try breaking your entire days' activities under these 4 heads, and look at scheduling your non sales Activities during the lean times.

<u>**EXERCISE**</u>
Break your day into 4 key areas, listing Activities and Time:

	Activities	Time
Planning:		
Prospecting:		
Selling:		
Administration:		

When planning your Day, it is a good idea to have a 'M.A.P.':
<u>M</u> ake a **daily 'To Do'** list of Key Activities
<u>A</u> ction   A Important AND Urgent ('must')
           B Important NOT Urgent ('should')
           C Urgent not Important ('could')
<u>P</u> rioritise A – B – C order daily

The How and What of Cold-Calling

For many, the term "cold calling" literally gives shivers and has many negative connotations and because of this many salespeople look for ways to avoid cold calling. Every company wants someone to make cold calls, but few have employees willing to do the 'dirty work'. Time after time, we've all seen even experienced sales people provide all excuses to avoid making such calls. Traditionally, it has been considered a painful part of the sales process, and rightly so, given the rejection, turn-downs, hang-ups and all the screening one has to go through. Typically, they're not interested in encountering those hundreds of rejections to find a few diamonds in the rough. The good news is that it doesn't have to be that way. You've probably seen people who are very successful in cold calling. Cold calling, in and of itself, is actually not the problem- it is the outlook and attitude that needs adjustment. Even with all the different methods out there to soften the approach, cold calling yet remains the most effective method to reach anyone you want to.

At the end of the day, you can remind yourself of two eternal rules of telemarketing:
1. *If you don't sell, you don't eat.*
2. *But if you continue to keep calling, you'll be upbeat and have a great treat!*

Aim of a cold call

The aim of any successful call must be 2 fold:
- Primary Objective: What you hope to achieve from the call
- Secondary objective: To leave a positive impression of your organization and ensure that the customer recalls and decides on your organization should there be any requirements in the future

So let's look at some primary objectives for your call.
These could be:
- To secure an appointment
- To close a deal/ obtain an order
- To collect an outstanding due
- To reactivate a dormant customer
- To inform and book into a seminar/ conference
- To work on restoring a sour relationship, particularly if the customer has had a problem or poor service
- To cross-sell another product or service
- To up-sell a more expensive item or an extended warranty or service
- To obtain information to update the database
- To find out the name of the decision maker, and other relevant information

Data for Cold Calling

Building on a good data bank of a potential audience is crucial for a successful telemarketing campaign. Therefore it must be emphasized on the importance of good prospect lists that are to be used and/or developed. Poor lists are a waste of time for the telemarketers, as they tend to reach the wrong people, causing poor public image for the company and frustration and de-motivation to the telemarketers

There are two basic types of lists:

- Compiled - lists of names taken from secondary sources such a phone directories, associations, chambers of commerce, other industrial directories etc.
- Responsive - lists of names of individuals/ companies that have responded in one way or another to some promotion (an advertisement of your company etc) or a mail out etc

Proper maintenance of Target Data

- Always identifying your target audience- Who are they?
- Break down your target audience into easily identifiable groups. This can help you prioritize your calls, your message/ script or presentation, help you measure your campaigns and get to understand what each group of customers specifically requires from you.
- The audience can be segregated: By size, turnover, number of employees, plants or factories, locations, outlets, by industry type or Standard Industrial Classification (SIC codes), or specialty fields such as automotive, construction, medical etc, or by geographical location, or by existing customers, or by dormant or past customers, or by warm leads etc
- Targeting is critical: It is pointless to contact consumers who are inappropriate for the product or service that you are promoting- it will increase your costs, lower your conversion rate and is likely to antagonize some people, including frustration amongst your own telemarketing team, and eventually affect your image in the market place. .
- When a prospect is called, notations should be made concerning the outcome of the sales call: a. Those that responded with a complete "NO" b. Those that wanted additional information c. Those that indicated some interest but did not purchase at this time d. Those that purchased at this time e. Others
- Maintain a master DNC (do-not-call) list: As a legal requirement (in most countries), you must maintain and consistently update in-house do-not-call (DNC) lists and ensure that this information is always shared amongst all members of the team. Often call lists are collated from a number of sources, and it is important to remember that these must always be run against your in-house DNC list. Your in-house DNC list must always be updated to include any 'do-not-call' requests made

Dealing with Gate-Keepers
Learning to make every gatekeeper a friend and not a foe!

Who are Gatekeepers?
Gatekeepers are people that act as a go-between, controlling access from one person to another. It's a person whose job it is to protect a decision maker's time, energy, and priorities. They are people whom you need to take permission to talk or to get to the key person. They may refuse, control or delay access to people or services. Whoever is acting as the gatekeeper between you and the key decision maker is just doing their job. Gatekeepers are a salesperson's greatest dread and that is probably why salespeople and gatekeepers don't usually blend well. On one hand, a salesperson is looking to get some meaningful time with a decision maker, while, the gatekeeper is there to keep away the uninvited distractions.
You will need to be aware of the fact that just as you are being trained on selling and cold calling, the gatekeeper is being trained on screening your cold calls. That is one of their key objectives, to reduce the number of unsolicited sales calls that come through the office. When you encounter those people we call the "Gatekeeper," they may not be your customer, but they know who is the customer- so bear in mind to be polite and respectful by remembering their name in your conversation.
The most powerful the person you want to speak with, the more chances of encountering a gatekeeper- and it could be a powerful gatekeeper too!

There are 3 types of 'gatekeepers'
- The Loyal Assistant: They report directly to the key person and could have roles such as Secretaries, Personal Assistants, Executive Assistants or Administrative Assistants. The stronger the loyalty factor, the greater the challenge to get past the gatekeeper
- Mid Level Managers: This person could come into the picture or scene often after you cross the initial gatekeeper (the loyal assistant) and they could report to the key decision maker. These people may be less driven by loyalty but much driven to creating the 'look good' factor in front of their key person
- The Imposter of Importance: This person is probably the toughest of all gatekeepers as he will always insist that you deal only with him directly. He is the one who projects power and authority far beyond what he actually possesses

Tips to make gatekeepers work for you
- Show respect and keep reinforcing how valuable they are: By treating the gatekeeper with respect, you show that you recognize their value and are committed to working with them, not around or above them.
- Use basic manners like please and thank you often along with their names
- Realize the fact that the gatekeepers are important in this entire deal
- Put yourself in the gatekeeper's shoes. Keep in mind that they are humans that are bombarded daily by vendors, clients, employees, stranger's etc- and they are just doing their part of the job

- If you tell them that you will only use five minutes of their time, then stick to those five minutes.
- Keenly look for opportunities where you can make their lives easier or better, either through your company's offerings or otherwise. It could mean just sharing an article of personal interest to the gatekeeper. (Eg; someone constantly suffering from migraines…provide tips to help relieve them of it!)
- Use the person's name: This signals you recognize the gatekeeper as beyond his/her role of an assistant or employee.
- Promote the gate keeper: Even if you know the title is that of a secretary, refer to the person as 'office manager' or 'executive advisor'. By doing so, he/she will not come up with an excuse that '*I am only an assistant here*'.
- Keep genuinely boosting their ego: It conveys that you rely on their knowledge alone and that they are extremely important to you.
- Be prepared for gatekeeper questions: A good telemarketer knows how much information to divulge and knows that you only divulge the minimum amount of information with each question.
  Example:
  Sarah Jackson please?
  Yes. Who is calling? – yes it's Gerard Assey, thank you…
  And from which company Mr. Assey? – From Sales Training India! Thanks….
  And what's it concerning? – Yes. Would you tell Sarah, it's with regards to………
  Thank you.

How to extract information from gatekeepers

- *"Is Mr. Jackson usually the one that handles decisions pertaining to….?"*
- *"You knowing Mr. Jackson so well, if you were me, how would you approach Mr. Jackson in this type of a situation?"*
- *"I know it could be challenging to anticipate every move, but when might be a good time to call him back?"*
- *"Is he usually available in the morning or the afternoon?"*
- *"You certainly know him very well. How does he approach decisions such as…?"*
- *"If you were in my shoes, what would you do?"*
- *"I know you are extremely busy, but could you advise me on…"*
- *"I would sincerely really appreciate your assistance".*
- *"I know your time is valuable, and I hesitate to ask you because of that, but could you please tell me…."*

Handling the Gatekeeper

Gate keepers often say that the decision maker is busy, and offer to take a message. And most often the message may not be passed on
So here are a few tips that you could try:

- *"I can appreciate that Mr. Jackson is busy and I know you are handling his schedule. Does he have 10 minutes of his time on Thursday or Friday when we could talk this over?"*

- *"I understand that his schedule is full and mine is full as well. In the interest of saving time, is he available on Thursday in the morning or afternoon to speak with me for 15 min?"*
- *"I realize Mr. Jackson is incredibly busy with meetings. Is it possible to get time on his calendar on a day when he is a little less booked?"*
- *"Okay, thank you. I realize it's your role to make sure Mr. Jackson is focused on the most important things and I value that. Can you please let Mr. Jackson know that Gerard Assey from Sales Training India called about (.........specific topic related to Mr. Jackson's known business challenges). In the meantime, if you can think of a better way for me to get him this information, I would sincerely appreciate your perspective."*

- Try not to leave messages with the Gatekeeper.
- Instead, find out a convenient time to call back. No one is sitting around waiting for you to call them and offer a product, service, or solution to a problem that they don't know they have. So sometimes the reception may be less than friendly.
- Call out of normal hours and lunchtime- the gatekeeper won't be there to protect the decision maker
- Sometimes calling before the company is officially open or half an hour after it officially closes can help. Many of these gatekeepers only keep to the official working hours of the company, but many supervisors and other staff start work earlier and leave later than these hours.
- Again, sometimes calling and asking to speak to somebody at helpdesk can be really helpful. Helpdesk staffs aren't trained to keep off sales personnel, and they're often only too happy to be helpful; it's in their job description after all.
- When an initial response is curt, ask permission to go forward. If it is denied, remain polite, apologize, and thank them for their time.

Working with scripts- The cold call
As customers, we have all experienced being sold to by someone who is obviously using a script. We can easily identify that they are not using their own words from the tone of their voice and the way the conversation flows. It can sometimes seem very canned and can put one off.
But a well written telephone script, if used the right way, can be a real asset to anyone in sales because:
- It can give you confidence and helps you stay in control
- It helps you focus on the structure of the call
- It helps to prevent you deviating, or saying the wrong thing
- It can sound so much more professional

Here are some tips on the preparation, use and effectiveness of scripts in cold calling:
Pre-call
- Set a specific time on a regular basis for cold calling. It is most effective to make your cold calls in blocks of time. You become more effective as you progress and

'warm up'. Try batch calling. Once you're in the groove of making calls, make a lot of them. You're likely to have all the information fresh in your mind. And you might even get more comfortable making those calls as you go.

- Review client information: Always do your researches first before you pick up a phone: Who are the people most likely to want to hear from you? And do they have the authority to take decisions? Will your call be relevant to them?
- Plan objective for the call- What do you want to achieve from these calls?
- Be mentally ready for the call! You must feel and sound confident. What you feel is what you get! On the phone your attitude, the words you use and your tone of voice are vital to your success. Think about what you are going to say and how you are going to say it
- Why should the customer bother to speak to you? What have you got that they need that they can't do themselves? Why would they use you if they already have a supplier of what you offer? Answers to these questions can help you be better prepared
- Know what you want to say: Write a script only as an outline; don't waste your time trying to memorize a "script".
- When writing your script, use your own words just as if you are having a normal relaxed conversation. Use spoken language rather than written language. Begin to write the script word for word for practice purposes.
- Practice by reading the script out loud to be sure it sounds professional. More practice with the script will allow the telemarketer to sound like a professional and not like they are reading the sales presentation to the customer.
- Highlight key words to use that are attention getters.
- Play the Numbers Game. You'll never do any business with someone you don't call. So, make enough calls to make the ratios work in your favor. That means focus and not becoming distracted by other tasks. Set a target for a day!

Checklist to have in front of you to be better prepared!
- Schedule of Calls for the Day
- Files/History Case Papers
- Documents pertaining to the accounts for the day
- Pens/ Note pad, Diary
- Script with Anticipated Questions/ Concerns
- Role Play/Rehearse your answers
- Smile/ Enthusiasm
- Business Appointment on time!
- Your mobile phone on silent or off mode
- Watch your mannerisms!
- Keeping your word!
- Body Language/Posture: Customer will not see you, but it shows in your voice!

The Call
- Block Your Time: Make or return phone calls at precisely the exact time you committed to. Don't even be 2-3 minutes late!

- Sound and feel confident - You've got something valuable to offer. Be articulate, pleasant and confident. After all, everyone is looking for ways to increase their business.
- Getting through the gatekeeper: (See details covered earlier on getting past gatekeepers)
- Getting to the decision maker: What will you say? How will you be able to get their attention to listen further?
- When introducing yourself, don't rush, especially when it comes to saying your name or that of your company's'. And don't avoid giving them your name. Let them know that you are a real person. Some telemarketers introduce themselves with things like: "Hello Logistics Department" People want to know your name. They want to speak with a real person, not a department.
- What are your opening statements going to be like? Because your call is unscheduled, you do not know what they are doing, when they answer their phone, and how focused they will be on what you are saying.
- Try not to speak too quickly but listen more by giving them opportunities to speak
- Your call opening should always contain the following information briefly but clearly:
  Who you are
  Where you are calling from
  The reason for your call (Why are you calling?)
  What's in it for them in listening to your call?
  You should ask "Is this a convenient time to speak?" and perhaps add that the call will take just X minutes and be sure it takes no longer
- Try not to use a 'Hi' or "Hello", but use a more professional salutation like a "Good Morning Mr…."
- Call the prospect by name
- Always try to follow up a statement with a question. This keeps you in control and helps put the customer at ease. Here is an example of what to say when cold calling: *"Good Morning, this is Gerard Assey from the Sales Training India. By the way, have you heard of us before?"* Customer may answer with a yes, or no. Whatever the case may be, here's a typical reply: *"Well as you are aware/you may not be aware, we specialise in training programs for sales personnel all across the globe, enabling them to be more successful by achieving greater results.* (Or *"we specialize in providing sales training solutions to help sales teams grow, thus enabling businesses to soar!") "Are you the person responsible for sales training at ABC Limited?"* The question gives you feedback and helps to make the call feel like a conversation, rather than a scripted attempt to con the other person into accepting an appointment
- *"The reason I am calling is to let you know of a powerful training program for your sales team that can help them close more deals and faster. I am sure you would like any good business, want to do so too?"* And so on.
- Asking questions and listening are the 2 most important skills in sales. Keep asking good open questions. These encourage the other person to talk and give you good quality information to work with.

- Qualify early in the call that they are the right person you should be talking to, instead of wasting time talking to the wrong person. What authority do they have? Are they in a position where they might be potential new customers? Have they bought in the past and might buy in the future?
- You could check if anyone else from their company should be included in the sales call. *"Would you like to have anyone else join us on this call?*
- A few open questions *like "What trainings have you done in the past?" "What was your experience like?" "How successful was it?"* and so on can open up to a lot of information.
- Gain general understanding of the client's business.
- Move from general to specific types of questions Ask questions to identify their needs and wants.
- Identify the customers' business need and generate a solution to match that need
- When you sell your company and its' products, or services sell benefits, not features. Convert features into benefits by saying ".this means that." For example: *"Our programs are tailored to meet your specific needs. This means that you can be sure that your team will be able to apply the learning to real life situations that they come across every day and bring in much better results and faster too"*
- Ask in-depth questions to test the feasibility of the solution.
- Prepare client for the recommendation.
- Present solution in a clear and concise manner.
- Keep using 'trial closes'. This means asking from time to time *"How does that sound?", "Is that the sort of thing you might be interested in?", "Would you like that?"* The purpose of trial closing is to gather feedback. We are not getting the order, but getting positive feedback that is making progress to the time when we ask for a commitment.
- Remember to talk of any additional up-sell or cross-sell opportunities ONLY if appropriate
- Ask for commitment. Don't be afraid to ask for some sort of commitment. 70% of salespeople fail to ask for commitment because they fear rejection.
- Summarize what has been discussed or agreed. Summaries are good for reminding the customer what has been discussed and agreed. It should include the following things: 1. Synopsis, for example: "Okay Mr X, so you would like to..." 2. Explain whom your customer's data will be passed to, and what action they will take 3. Ask your customer if they are happy to receive email, phone or mail contact in future 4. Thank your customer sincerely for their time and end the call
- If your customer has no apparent need or desire for your product or service, you MUST conclude your call professionally and politely.
- Respect that even where no sale is made, a good customer experience will spread a positive perception of your company and the brand you are promoting and will eventually encourage the customer to come back some day when there is a need and help them draw more customers and long-term market share for you.

- Ending your call with an action plan is vital to ensure that your customer is clear about the outcome of your call and to ensure that there has been no misunderstanding about what will happen next.
- Always ask for a testimonial or letter of satisfaction that you can use with other similar customers
- Thank client for the business.
- Always leave name, telephone number and email id.
- End each call on a positive note, as people are most likely to remember the last thing you say

(Note: A Detailed method to go about structured calls is covered in the chapters that follow)

Post-Call

- Post-call process: Fulfill your commitments or promises made during a call within the timescale agreed with your customer- do not promise things that cannot be delivered upon
- Have a system to practice your scripts with your supervisor, friends and colleagues with every opportunity you get, as the more you practice, the more confident you get, enabling you to rely less on the actual script itself. And as you keep progressing, keep refining your script based on feedback and inputs received from the ones close to you.
- Measure your activity. Good record keeping is vital to building your database and measuring your success rates. Take a bit of time to review what happened and talk to colleagues if you need help.
- Keep going. You will get rejection. It may take several calls before they say yes, but your persistence will pay off. Reward yourself when the session is finished and review your results so you can plan for next time.

Finally, learn to make telephone selling a daily habit, and you will begin to enjoy it and you will find yourself with more appointments or closures than you ever imagined.

Telemarketing Campaigns
Campaign Planning

Know your goals!

You have to know exactly what you want from any campaign. For example is it an increase in sales, increase in enquiries or increased knowledge about your customer base? You also need to know what targets you have set and how you are going to measure and evaluate the results.

So when running a telemarketing campaign there are a few objectives to keep in mind:

- What do you want to achieve from this campaign?
- How will your campaign benefit your customer? What's in it for them?
- Are your objectives achievable and measurable? Specifically what are they?
- How are your telemarketers going to help achieve the objectives? Action plan!
- How many calls will be required to be made/ how many decision makers contacted?

- How will you obtain/ source this list?
- Research to fully profile and understand your potential customers and their needs. Define the ideal profile of your customer, enabling you to approach them effectively.
- What are the realistic conversion rates expected/ achievable?
- Match telemarketers -Whenever possible, select telemarketers who have a genuine interest in the product they will be promoting, as this will help enhance customer confidence and promote a genuine conversation rather than a scripted one.
- In addition to revenue, what other quality objectives should you look at?
- Apply any learning's from previous campaigns or industry research
- During this campaign, what valuable customer insight can you collect during each call and how will this insight be used to help improve your customer's experience in future campaigns?

Campaign monitoring

- You should always evaluate the effectiveness of any campaign. If it isn't working in its current format there is no point in continuing. You should make sure that your evaluation methods are set up before your campaign begins
- Review campaign daily after 24 hours of calling
- Check against objectives, that your campaign is achieving your original objectives
- Have ways to monitor customer dissatisfaction levels if any and evolve your campaign to minimize these.
- Watch for conversion rate drops and peaks in specific segments, for each telemarketer, day, time etc, this can help you set future objectives.
- Know when to stop running the campaign to avoid increased customer dissatisfaction.
- Get constant feedback from your telemarketers on reaction/ feedback of customers
- Keep building on and implementing every days new learning's

Selling to B2B/ Key Accounts
The Selling Process- The 6 Step Selling Plan outline

From this chapter onwards, we will be covering how to sell to B2B/ Key Accounts, using a structured 6 step selling plan. But before we go any further, let us ask ourselves: What is 'Selling'? What comes to your mind when you hear the word 'Selling' or 'Sale'?
I can guarantee you that for most sales people, the very first words that pop up in our minds would be words like *revenue, profits, quotas, targets, etc*…all related to money! Shouldn't this then only confirm what came up in the survey (that we seen earlier) on 'What customers hate about Sales People'? We are more concerned with what is in the customers' wallet, his checkbook or the order, than genuinely helping the customer.
But if we could change that thinking to a feeling that Selling is more of *'Problem Solving'*, it would then change our entire perspective of the selling process and the way we treat the customer particularly. Let us now change that 'hat' that we have been wearing from a Sales Person to that of a Consultant or Advisor! Someone has a problem and our job is to genuinely help that person get out of that problem or situation, then only will our whole perception towards the selling process change.

It is like what happens when a patient visits a doctor. A genuine doctor, will never prescribe, until he has really diagnosed the problem completely. When this happens the customers' confidence and respect for the sales person zooms up. He now begins to trust you as the sales person, thus leading to rapport and a lasting relationship

If you look at the word 'SALE' – the word actually tells you in an acronym the steps that one should follow. Most times, a sales person, just rushes into providing his pitch on the product or service that he represents, without actually taking time to understand the need of a customer. This acronym should be a reminder for us to…
STOP (think!)
Ask Questions (to understand the need of the customer),
Listen to understand…and finally
Engage, Enthuse and Excite the customer, by letting the customer do more of the talking

The Foundation of the Sales Process
What do you think could be the reason that makes someone buy from a Particular Company or Salesperson?
You will be surprised to note that most times, the reason is neither the product, nor the price, but rather the **relationship** with the person with whom they're dealing.
Products will change, services will change, prices will change, economies and market places will change too- but if the relationship is strong, the account endures.
I have seen many accounts move as the sales person moved from the company too.
The only thing that truly matters is the relationship between the seller and the buyer.

When you don't have an edge in product technology or price, then you need an edge in the way you <u>connect</u> with people.

The foundation of Relationship is an important word: TRUST. To make a buying decision, a customer has to make a leap of faith. Successful telemarketers create a safety net called trust. Trust helps your customers take that leap in complete confidence.

This is what Relationship or Consultative Selling can do. Unlike the Hard Sell Approach, in relationship or collaborative selling, the telemarketer takes time up front to build a sincere, committed relationship by investing time in learning about the customer's needs. Then, every step of the sales process that follows is conducted with the relationship in mind. This ensures an enduring and lasting relationship, leading to repeat business and referrals

The Structured Call: The 6 Step Selling Cycle

From this module, we would be entering into the Selling Cycle comprising of 6 steps:

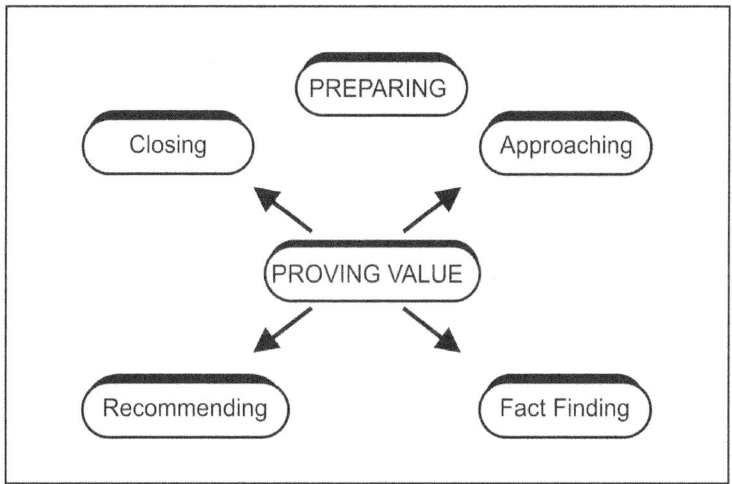

You will notice in the illustration that there are 6 steps to Professional Selling-at a glance. If you were asked to pick the 3 most important steps according to you, what do you think they would be? Go ahead have a guess, before I provide what I believe are the 3 'most-important-never-to-skip' steps! (What comes up from you?)

While ever step is important, these 3 are the 'most-important-never-to-skip' steps!

1. Preparation
2. Fact-finding
3. Proving Value

But distressingly, a good majority of the 'so called sales people' out there totally skip these three steps and move into the other three steps of Approaching, Recommending and Closing. They greet the customer, and then believe they know or assume his need (as the sales lead could have been through an enquiry or referral) and so now because of the mismatch of the customers' real need and the sales persons assumed need, there is now a struggle to close.

This could be a total 'put-off' for the customer. The sales person has no right to recommend, without uncovering the customers' exact need or problem.

From the 6 Step Selling Cycle illustration, you will notice that there are 2 interesting points...Did you notice that the step of Preparing is isolated from the other 5 steps...And do you know why?

For two major reasons: Because this is done before you pick up the phone to talk to the client-and the other reason is that, this is the step that can set the tone for a positive outcome. You have no right to a customer's time if you aren't prepared. If you want someone to have confidence and invest several dollars with you in business, then in all fairness we need to do some work upfront. This also helps you stand out from the competition. ..The Customer feels confident dealing with someone who cares!

The other interesting point that stands out is the fact that Proving Value is placed right in the centre of the others...Reason being...Everything you say revolves or centers on the perceived value of your product or service in the eyes of the customer

The average sales person out there usually spends less or no time at all in trying to understand the need of the customer, and because of which ends on a mismatch when providing the solution. It's a solution that may not usually match the need and hence the sales person always has objections that he has to encounter and because of which may eventually lose a sale together with credibility!

However, with the Consultative Approach the sales person spends a lot of time up front in trying to unravel the specific need of the customer. When this happens there is now a clear match with the solution provided. It leads to both the customer and sales person working as partners, building trust along, where the customer is involved in the solution, thus bringing down the objections that the traditional telemarketer faces.

Preparing and Planning your Call

The First Step- Preparation
The first step in the Consultative Selling Skills Cycle is **Preparation.**
As preparation is the first step in the selling plan, it can as such, be likened to the foundation of the call. **Preparation is vital, as it provides the research required to pursue an intelligent and productive interview.**

Before we go any further into this, let us first ask: Why Prepare?
- *Makes you feel more confident*
- *You are able to discuss intelligently*
- *Saves time – yours and the customer*
- *Get to understand customer potential needs*
- *Become more aware of business*
- *Prepare a good recommendation*
- *Study competition*
- *Your customers respect for you goes up*
- *Professional in the eyes of the customer*
- *Customer knows you have called to help- not extract*
- *You are proving that you are unlike other telemarketers*

A telemarketer has no right to call a customer if he/she hasn't prepared for the account. On the other hand, when a customer experiences that the telemarketer is prepared; his respect for the sales person and the company that he represents zooms up.
How fair is it to a customer when a sales person tries to solicit business that is worth several thousands or millions of money, without doing any groundwork for the customer? When a customer is going to part with several thousands of his money, shouldn't you as a sales person do some amount of ground work before contacting him. This is what will lead to respect, resulting in enhanced credibility and a lifelong relationship, because now the customer can see clearly that you, as the sales person are genuinely interested in helping him, and not just after his money!

A lot of people think that Selling has a lot to do with 'being lucky'!
My answer is that 'Good Selling' is not a 'matter of Luck', but rather a combination of Preparation plus Opportunity where Preparation accounts for 99%. Now when 99% of efforts have been put in, and that 1% opportunity gets by you, then that is what will make you the so called 'lucky person'
But if you are unprepared and that 1% opportunity comes by, it will just go past you and move to someone more prepared. That is why preparation is the key to a successful sale. I call it being an 'Eagle System Seller' and just as how an Eagle is focused and watchful, an Eagle System Seller spends more than 55% on this step alone, as he prefers to 'prepare than repair' or have any regrets later.

Analyzing Accounts

Before you start to prepare on an individual account, you would need to analyze the different accounts assigned to you or in your territory so this could help you prioritize your sales calls.

In the 1st illustration below, you could list your accounts in the boxes that best correspond to the combinations of '**Sales Volume**' and **'Profits'.** Your goal should be to work your accounts so they move up in 'Sales Volume' and 'Profitability'.

ANALYZE YOUR ACCOUNTS

SALES VOLUME

	Low	Medium	High
High			
Medium			
Low			

PROFITABILITY

The next step would be to classify your accounts in terms of 'Profitability' and prioritizing them to determine how and when to call on them. Using the 2nd illustration below, you could use the data from your past (last one year) and rank your accounts by their profitability. You could do this separately for each product line or service.

ANALYZE YOUR ACCOUNTS

	Company	Contact	Phone
"A" Accounts Top 20% Very Profitable			
"B" Accounts Middle 30% Profitable			
"C" Accounts Bottom 50% Less Profitable			
PROSPECTS			

Preparing for Individual Accounts

The step of Preparation for an individual account, involves compiling and analyzing relevant client information and developing an appropriate sales call strategy on how to handle the customer

The Purpose of Preparing is to have an overview of the client's current status with your company (as a new or existing customer), the competition, the industry and marketplace which will allow you to approach him in an appropriate way.

Being the first and key part in the Consultative Selling Cycle, it consists of **5 key steps**:

The 1ˢᵗ step is all about preparing yourself-the mental and physical self, which we have already covered in an earlier module

The 2ⁿᵈ Step is preparing information related to the customer…things like,

Who is the contact person or decision maker?

What business is your prospect in?

Who are your prospect's competitors?

Who are they currently dealing with and for how long?

How happy are they with this set up,

How does your prospect make money?

How do they pay?

What are the challenges your prospect faces?

What is your prospect concerned about day after day?

What problems or concerns can you help the prospect address and solve?

How can your product(s)/service(s) help your prospect earn more money, save money, save time, reduce stress, or alleviate a concern?

These are just a few thoughts. You could build your own checklist in the exercise that follows.

The 3ʳᵈ Step is all about the Market, the Industry and the Competition….Examples would be:

What is the market like?

Who are the other players?

Where does your organization stand in relation or comparison with them?

What are their USP's etc?

How does your company or products compare with the competition- the strengths/ weaknesses etc?

The more details you have, you will be in a better position when talking with the customer.

The 4ᵗʰ Step is about what you need to keep always ready in front of you on this call that can help you…things like, pens that write, note pad, pdf files of your brochures, pricelists, testimonials etc that you can email soon after the call.

And finally the **5ᵗʰ Step** is your Call Strategy…How and when are you planning on making this first contact- your approach, what are you going to say, what are the questions you are planning to ask to uncover the customers' need , what are the type of concerns you could expect and how would you go about handling them.

Basically this 5ᵗʰ step is more of a role play of the entire call in your mind before calling the customer that would actually set you up for success. Obviously you will be more confident with doing this 5th step only after you have covered all steps of this 6 step selling plan

Depending on the market you are in and the customer; 'selling on credit' could be a very important decision. If your company's policy is to sell on credit in your market, then one of the key areas you'd like to keep in mind before you get the customer into your fold is to assess his creditworthiness or his ability to pay you…and on time!

Now this takes several checks…and given below are some suggestions to help you.

- *Past Records.*
- *Sales Representatives Reports (In House Opinion)*
- *Bank Reference.*
- *Trade Associations.*
- *Chambers Of Commerce.*
- *Credit Rating Agencies.*
- *Visit to Customers Premise.*
- *Market Feedback.*
- *Press Reports.*
- *Directorate of Foreign Trade*
- *Registrar Of Companies (Annual Reports)*
- *Customers Suppliers/ Service Providers*
- *Stock Exchange Opinion.*
- *Life of Business.*
- *Nature f Business.*
- *Reference Checks*
- *Family Background*
- *Assets*
- *Website*

You don't have to check into all of these areas, but a good indicative way or thumb rule would be if you find 4 to 5 areas positive, it should tell you that the road is fairly clear to move ahead…but if you do have a few red areas, then you will need to do further probing or investigation on the customers standing in the market.

Remember: As sales people the temptation is always for more business without having to carry out such checks. However, prevention is better than cure! One rotten apple can mess your entire basket soon…Word travels fast! So treat this step with caution.

Another checklist you as a telemarketer would like to build up on is the items in your kit to keep ready before calling. A suggested sample list is what you see below…however start building your own.

- *Diary/ Note Pad*
- *Pens that write*
  All of the below items in soft copy format:
- *Visual aids/Brochures*
- *Testimonials*
- *Best Rates*
- *Competition Statistics*
- *News Articles*

- *Proposal*
- *PPT Presentation for larger corporates…etc*

Customers like to deal with organized people that do not waste their time. Also if the customer notices you as being organized, his respect for you will go up, while being assured that his business would also be handled in an orderly way! Nobody would want to deal with someone who is messy or disorganized.

When preparing it is a good idea to: Think of 4 Cs
Customer, **C**ompetitor, **C**apabilities, and **C**ost (Value)

Customer:
- *Do they know us? What information do they have about us?*
- *Do we know them in any way? What information do we have about them?*

Competitor:
- *Who are the Competitors?*
- *What are their positions in the eyes of the customer?*
- *How does the customer see/ perceive them?*
- *Brainstorm their Strengths/Weaknesses*
- *Has an examination of your competitors' strengths or weaknesses uncovered sufficient reason to warrant re-examination of your initially selected strategy*
- *What aspects of the requirement which (from your knowledge of your competition) you can speculate your competitor will address more effectively than you.*
- *Is there any impact on your selected strategy? It is important that you re-examine your selected strategy again- in the light of your competitors' strengths and weaknesses.*
- *Is there anything area that weakens your case sufficiently for you to consider a change of strategy?*

Capabilities:
- *What are our capabilities?*
- *Do we stand out from the competition? In what areas?*

Cost (Value)
- *What value are we bringing to the customer? How would he view it?*

Preparing for Existing Customers!
When preparing for existing customers, you might like to keep the following in mind:
- *Analyze any weaknesses in your solution*
- *Are there any show-stoppers?*
- *Are there any points that will render the selected strategy ineffective? If so, then reconsider your decision on strategy*

Study Past Successes- Some Generic Strategies
Cost
You might well have won the business for one of the following reasons:
Lowest price or best price/performance or (ROI)
Technical Aspects
In this instance the lead decision-maker was most likely a senior technical officer in the client organisation. You may have won because of: superior specifications or program/ solution design, or better technical personnel.
Quality
A quality orientation can manifest itself in either of two ways: "Snob" value or proven high quality/reliability.
Competitiveness
There are 2 ways you may have found your proposals were successful:
The extent to which you proved that your solution was vastly superior to that of any of your competition, or the extent to which you convinced your client that your solution would afford them some significant competitive edge over their own competition.
Credibility
Whether the lead decision-maker was technically, financially or administratively oriented, the credibility of your organisation could have been a compelling argument for or against your proposal. You could have been selected because of: Who your organisation is or your team members or industry experience.

EXERCISE
Now try making your own Checklist before going to meet the customer:
A. Self- Mental/ Physical
B. Client Info: (including Creditworthiness)
C. Market/ Industry/ Competition Information
D. Sales Tools

Note, that we are not doing an exercise on the 5th Step which is 'Call Strategy' as this can be done only after you know or have covered all the other steps of the sales process.
So as can be seen, for you to be an effective Sales Person you will need to work on being organized and have **SYSTEMS**. When you do have **SYSTEMS**, you will find that it will help…
Save
You
Stress
Time
Energy
Money and…
Sleepless Nights!
While also enhancing your credibility and productivity!

At this stage of the Sales Cycle, it is important as a Professional Telemarketer to try and understand the mind of the buyer

The key Rule is to always try to find out where or at which phase of the buying process the client is currently in:

If in phase 1- then we are First-Great!

Good to be No.1, as people tend to remember those first. (Example; If I asked you who was the 1st person to climb Mount Everest or go to the moon- you would certainly know the answer. But very rarely or we may find it difficult remembering the 2nd or 3rd person that did so!)

If in phase 2- then we may not be First!

Let us look at Phase 1- if we are first. It is important for us to determine his needs and obviously there could be 4 stages to put across, in a simplified manner

1. They need something
2. Rough idea-What would it be/ look like?
3. Rough cost- Affordability?
4. Finally…the sources-Who can help them?

Now that the customer has the various sources in front of him, he enters Phase 2 wherein he begins to evaluate the options in front.

In other words what's best for his company and where can he avail the services from?

He now moves to Phase 3 which involves Evaluating of Risks in doing business with a new supplier. Right on top of his mind, would in most times be the 'Quality of Service' followed by the 'Rate or Pricing'.

A point to note is that price can never stand alone and is always related to quality. The next area that the client would probably evaluate is if your prices match his current budgets set for this. Here is where transparency is very important where he would like to have a clear break up of your working.

Lastly, the customer would like to consider the fact that should the vendor mess up at some stage, then how would the vendor handle such situations?

This is where having a good list of satisfied customers can help, with words like:

"If you don't believe me-Ask my clients!" (A third and independent opinion is always helpful and important)

Approaching Customers

The Second Step in the Consultative Selling Cycle is Approach
Approaching is the **second step** in the Consultative Selling Cycle and is the process of making your first or initial contact with a client. The initial customer contact is an important part of the interview as it "sets the tone" or establishes the climate for the rest of the interview.
Beginning the interview, the sales person should anticipate a few potential customer deterrents to buy:
Apprehensions about the Telemarketer
Apprehensions about the Company
Apprehensions about the Product
Buyer's Resistance
Price Concerns

At this stage, therefore, the sales person should be sensitive to the customer's apprehension about him/herself and the company. So the purpose of the Approach step is to build rapport and provide an opportunity to move to the next step to uncover client needs ie; to help you to move to the next step in the Consultative Selling Cycle which is Fact Finding.
There are three types of approaches we could use in making initial contact with a client:

- The Telephone
- Face-to-face (Premise)
- or E-mail

Regardless of which approach is used, the initial contact should contain basically three vital elements:

- A reason for contacting the client
- An indication of the next step you plan to take
- A request for action

Since the objective of this book is on Telemarketing, we'd like to particularly concentrate on the telephone approach. In terms of both the **content** (the words used) and the **style** (the way in which the content is delivered) an effective approach consists of three parts:

- The Introduction
- The Body and the
- The Close

We have seen in an earlier module how Communication takes place with Words, Tone and Body Language. Now when it comes to communicating over the telephone, the most important percentage of 55% which comes from body language will be missing, with only 45% part being active with your Words and Tone. This means that our communication is only 45% effective if not done carefully. Therefore in order to compensate for this missing 55% we would need to work on our enthusiasm levels with our 'attitude' and 'voice modulation'. (See details on tone aspects covered in earlier chapter)

The introduction must cover 5 key components:
The salutation
Your name
Your company (that you represent)!
One line about what your company does- An attention grabber!
Check convenient time
Your purpose of calling

You begin by wishing the customer, then identifying yourself first and then stating the name of your company, followed by one key point on what your company does relevant to this customer's interest. (An important point to note here is to try and not use a *'Hi'* or *'Hello'* as a salutation- this sounds very unprofessional. A real professional approach would be a *'Good Morning, Afternoon or Evening'* as the case may be) Next check to see if you have called at a convenient time. If not, ask when it would be more convenient.
Explain the purpose of the call.
The Body is one of the trickiest parts, and is also referred to as using an 'ICR' or Interest Creating Remark. In fact, this part can make your call stand out from the several other calls that your customer will be receiving for the day. And if you can master how to do this, you will be able to gain entries into most places. It is based on the principle that people like to hear or talk more about themselves than want to listen to others. Keeping this in mind, it is important to do a little bit of research earlier. Find out what is something new or exciting happening currently at the customers organization. It could be that they have bagged an award, or you'd seen an article about their growth or expansion plans, or an article about their CEO. Something is always happening in every organization. We only need to be interested. Use this to commend, congratulate or appreciate them. It can do wonders! This also gives them the feeling that you care about them and are aware of what is happening and not there only for their money! Surprisingly, this helps them be more open now to what you've got to say!
Once you've got their attention, you now ask if it would be ok for you to ask a few questions in order to better understand their business, gradually moving them to the next step of the Selling Cycle.

A simple example would be as follows:
'Good Morning/ Afternoon' Mr. So and So (Sir or Mr, as the case may be, or whatever you are most comfortable with, though I recommend using the Customers' name) 'This is 'Gerard Assey calling from Citius, Altius, Fortius Unlimited.
As you are probably aware, we are an over 19 year old leading international training company, with presence in 6 countries' specializing in providing training solutions to help your people grow, thus enabling your business soar!
Before I go any further Mr So and So, I'd like to check to see if I've called you at a convenient time (or you may like to also use… *'Is it a good time to talk to you?'*)
'The purpose in me calling you this (morning or afternoon as the case may be) Mr. So and So, *is to see how we could work along with you in providing a solution to some of your training and human resource challenges'.*

(Don't talk anything more-This becomes the 'Intro' part of your Approach)
The Body is one of the trickiest parts as explained earlier and if done well can help see you making an entry really easy. As an example you could say something like… *'Oh by the way, before I go any further, Congratulations on that new plant you've opened in Malaysia…We were so happy to read about this in the news! "*
Now this has to be done with a lot of enthusiasm and a genuine feeling of excitement. And the moment you say something that concerns them you've got their attention. Their usual reaction would be something like… *'Oh when or where did you see that news article? Can I get a copy?"* or *'Thanks a lot…yes we've got some new challenges ahead now with this latest project on hand"*
Whatever be their response, you've got their attention at this stage.
We now move to the 'Close' part of this step, by saying something like: *'In order for me to better understand your business, could I take a few minutes of your time to ask you a few questions that will help me better understand it.*
Also I'd like to take some notes as we go along…Is it ok with you?"

(Note: This last line of asking to take notes- even though on phone and the customer can't see you do so, is vital! It subtly tells the customer that you are interested and you are there to help him. The competitor that called earlier did not do this- they were more interested in getting the business!)

EXERCISE
Using the structure explained above, work on your own script for the Approach Step. Once you've written it, role-play it a few times in your mind, till you get the flow and gain confidence.
Introduction: (Cover the 5 points mentioned above)
Body: (The Interest creating remark!)
Close: (Permission to move to the next step: Fact-finding!)

What we just covered above is an example of approaching a new customer. But for existing customers you might prefer a different approach that could start off by building further…
1. Rapport: (Start with something pleasant and interesting to the customer!)
You could then get into your…
 2. Introduction: By saying something like: *'Thank you for providing me your time today…What I'd like to do in the next 10 minutes is…*
a) Share information on our company
b) You and your situation
c) Mutually see whether worthwhile continuing
Is that ok as an agenda for you?
(For particularly old clients you might like to share some new developments of your company)
And in case 'you' are new to contacting this old client of your company, you might want to add *'…and I have been with* (name your company) *for the past ….'* (to build confidence)
"Enough about me, now tell me about you and your situation"

Now before we go deep into the third step which is Fact-Finding, it is important that we invest some time in trying to see who the key decision makers are or what is the typical decision making process. The earlier the better! Studies show that sales people make several calls only to realize later that they wasted their precious time talking to the wrong people or to somebody that did not have the authority to take things forward.

You need to identify all those involved in the decision-making chain.
- *Who all are involved?*
- *Their Roles- Purpose of their job?*
- *Their Responsibility- What is the main function of job-holder*
- *Authority level- Who ultimately has the power to sign-off limits*

Key Points to Understanding the Decision Process
- *WHO? Who will decide on this Order/ Tender/ Bid/ Contract/ Award?*
- *WHAT? What is their decision making criteria?*
- *WHY? Why will they base their decision on that?*
- *WHEN? When will they be involved?*
- *WHERE? Where do they have influence?*
- *HOW? How can I positively influence them?*

You could use any of the following 3 acronyms to help you remember how to Qualify Customers?

W.A.N.T.S. Framework
- ***W**ants- Exactly what are they looking for?*
- ***A**uthorities- Decision making process- What level of influence do they have on making decisions?*
- ***N**eeds- Organisational goals- Does the prospect have a need worth solving?*
- ***T**imescales- Evaluation and implementation- How soon they need a solution?*
- ***S**pend Capacity- Budget and when available- Do they have or can they find the ability to spend money on solving these challenges?*

The B.A.N.T. Framework
- ***B**udget: Is the prospect capable of buying?*
- ***A**uthority: Does your contact have adequate authority to sign off on a purchase?*
- ***N**eed: Does the prospect have a business pain you can solve?*
- ***T**imeline: When is the prospect planning to buy?*

The F.A.I.N.T. Framework
- ***F**unds- Money?*
- ***A**uthority- Decision, Key Authority?*
- ***I**nterest- Eagerness, Desire?*
- ***N**eed- Pain area?*
- ***T**iming- When?*

Now here's an **important tip** that top sales people use in case the customer requires you to call back later…and just before you could put down the phone…

Always assign your prospect some 'Homework' on 'Uncovering Pain Areas':
Give your prospect some homework before the appointment. You could begin by saying the following:
"Mr. Prospect. In order to make our next call as productive as possible, would you make a list of the two or three most challenging issues you are having with respect to …..? Then we can really focus our discussion on these issues and try to develop a solution. Does that make sense?"

Fact-Finding: Uncovering the Needs and Pains of Customers

The Third and another very important step as mentioned earlier, is the 'Fact-finding' or 'Uncovering of Needs' Stage. This step and the next which is Proving Value can really make that big difference between you and the competition.

Fact Finding is the process of uncovering the client' needs, problems, opportunities or pain areas by which can be solved by the products or services of your company.

The purpose of Fact Finding is to obtain information that will allow you to move to the next step which is Proving Value

The extent to which Fact Finding is effectively completed will significantly impact the outcome of the next steps in the Consultative Selling Cycle

When trying to unravel needs, it must be done in a logical pattern that will bring the customer to a stage of realization that there is a problem or need.

So the art of uncovering needs requires the use of different types of questions. First let us have an understanding of the different types of questions that we could ask someone. Though there are several types of questions, for the purpose of this exercise let us look at just the 2 most important ones ie;

OPEN Questions

CLOSED Questions

Depending on what type of answer you want from the other person, either of these questions are used.

Eg; If I asked you: *'Did you have your dinner'?*

Or *'Do you like this training session?'* or *'Are you going home this evening'?*

The only possible answer that you could give me would either be a *'yes'* or a *'no'*

That is why this type of Question is called a 'closed Question', because the only possible answer would be a one word- with either a *'yes'* or *'no'*

Closed questions usually begin with:

'Are you…'

'Will you…'

'Do you…'

'Would you…'

They are usually not very helpful in starting a conversation and extracting information. However, most sales people are more comfortable asking such questions, which we need to avoid at this stage.

The opposite of 'closed' is the obvious: 'open'.

Open questions allow the customer to open up or do the talking and are used to encourage a client to speak freely about a concern or expand on something already raised during the conversation

Always remember this: Open Questions generally begin with 5W's and 1 H ie;

Who?

What?

When?
Where?
Why?
How?
And they encourage the other person to open up and speak.

If we were to redo that example again using open questions, they would go something like this: *'What did you have for dinner?' 'How do you feel about this training?' 'What plans do you have for this evening'?*

These questions will certainly not fetch you a *'yes'* or *'no'* like how closed questions do. But they would allow the other person to open up with information which is what you as a sales person require.

Shooting out these questions without any logical order would also be inappropriate, as it could be unprofessional, could be irritating at times and most of all cause confusion in the mind of the customer. But if the customer was taken through a logical pattern, it could help lead him or open up to an understanding of his own situation, problem or need- that many times he may not be aware of.

There are two methodologies that could be used. Either of them is fine and would depend on which one you get more comfortable with. We recommend though, that the first method be used for simple, non complicated accounts, whilst the second method be used for complicated or major accounts.

The logical pattern for the first method mentioned usually starts with his **'Current Situation'** …Questions like *'Where is the client now, Who is he dealing with, for how long and how satisfied is he'?*

This is where they are **'now'**. These questions are at most times factual and the answers to these are most times available either on their websites or from others around and are used to help start the conversation and build rapport. So we usually recommend that we do not ask many of these.

We then gradually move to the **'Desired Situation'** of where does the customer want to be or should be, with Questions like *'What would they like the ideal service levels to be or What would they like to see or have from an ideal vendor'*. The answers to these questions will tell us the customer's future plans or where they should be or want to be.

The next set of questions, are pertaining to the **'Barriers'** that are in his way, that are preventing him from reaching the desired situation. This is the key that will enable him open his eyes. Sometimes, just one question here could open up opportunities. Barrier questions most times begin with: *'What is preventing you from… "What is stopping you from…What is coming in the way to…"*

Here are some examples of these 3 types of Questions:
Current:
What are your upcoming projects?
What is the current status of the project?
How long have you been dealing with this service provider?

Desired:
What are your customer's expectations?

How happy are you with the service of the existing provider and what would you like it to be?
What are your expectations in having these resolved?
How do you plan to address these issues?
What would you like to happen to ensure a smooth working?

Barriers:
What are the factors coming in the way of you creating/maintaining a good brand Image?
What are the factors stopping you from maintaining a problem free situation?
What are the parameters which are preventing you to achieve…..?

EXERCISE
Now keeping your customer in mind, look at building at least 5 questions each for 'Current' and 'Desired' and maybe 3 for 'Barriers
Current
Desired
Barriers

The second method as mentioned earlier is the **C.O.R.K.** Model- which we would normally recommend for large or key accounts; **C.O.R.K.** standing for: **C**urrent Circumstances, **O**bstacles, **R**epercussions and **K**ey for Solution
You could start with the current situation on the Circumstances or Factual Questions, to help you start building a rapport to move on. Caution again here is not to ask too many of these Questions, since these are factual and it may seem or give the impression that you have not done prior work…So limit it to a few just to help you get started.

The next set of questions are the ones that can help open up on the Obstacles or Problems your customer is currently facing. Most times the customer will not even realize that they are sitting on a problem! Sometimes for years they could be living with this pain or problem without realizing. This is the real pain that his company could be going through. So effective Questions here can help him open up on this pain.

The third set of Questions deal with the Repercussions that these pains or problems could have or cause or lead to if not handled on time or not handled now! This creates the urgency for a change now! This is the subtle fear part that will help the customer make a change or decide to listen further to you.

The fourth set of Questions- the 'Key for Solution' is the step of asking the customer of what they think a good solution might be, which helps in promoting a platform for your solution and gain commitment from them on the usefulness of this proposed solution from you.

These four questions could be around the following key areas depending on your products or services:
- The Contacts or Decision Makers or Purchasing Process
- Current Supplier/Pricing

- Needs (long term/volume)
- The Organization size
- Special Delivery Requirements
- The Decision Making process
- Problems with Current Supplier (the Pain!)
- Problems this causes with other departments
- Other Problems

By being thorough in the preparation of your questions , which is usually done in advance at your preparation stage, you can ensure that nothing is missed and you can move to the next stage of the sales process with all the information you need.

We just covered a little earlier about the C.O.R.K. Model of Questioning. But I'd like to spend some more time on the 3 most important parts of this model- the **Obstacles,** the **Repercussion,** and **Key for Solution** set of Questions

Obstacle Questions are all about unraveling or probing about concerns, problems, pains, dissatisfactions or difficulties that the buyer is experiencing with the existing situation

Examples of this type of Question would be:

'What makes this operation difficult'?

'In what areas are you experiencing most difficulties'?

'What are some of the challenges you are experiencing with your existing supplier'?

Repercussion Questions are about the **consequences or effects** of a buyer's problems, difficulties, or dissatisfactions.

Once you have an indication or picture of the type of problem the customer is going through, you would now need to build or draw the customers' attention to the Repercussion or Effect that this problem could have if not acted on time.

Examples of this type of Question would be:

'What effect does that problem have on output (or on your customers/ market)?

'Could that lead to added costs'?

'What happens if you do not achieve that goal'?

'Which other departments are effected'? Or 'Who all are effected with this'?

As you will see from the discussion that you have with the customer, several Implications can lead from one overriding problem or issue. Linking other possible problems or consequences to a given problem clearly increases its significance and urgency to the Buyer.

The 'Key for Solution' Questions will help you to get your customers to tell you the benefits that your solution can offer by asking them what they think a good solution might be, which can further help promote a platform for your solution and gain commitment from them on the usefulness of this proposed solution from you, when you move to the next step (Proving Value) of the Selling Cycle.

Examples of this type of Question would be:

'If you had to do ...., by how much would that save you'?'

'What would it mean to your customer service if you could have ....fitted or done'?

'What would it mean to your image and customer service if you could have……?

Here are some examples of the C.O.R.K. Model of Questions…focusing on the Current Circumstances, The Obstacles and the Repercussions. I hope that this will help give you a start in building your own list.

Circumstance Questions (Factual and most times can be used to build rapport-But don't waste time asking too many. These can usually be picked up from elsewhere prior to your meeting!)

- *What areas do you operate in?*
- *How many people work here?*
- *What is the ideal decision making process?*
- *What areas are you hoping to expand to?*

Obstacle Questions (Important!)

- *What criteria do your customers judge you on?*
- *What are the difficulties in working with....?*
- *Have you ever had a situation where you......*
- *What were some of the issues you've had to face in the past?*
- *What are issues you are facing in catering to your customer's expectations?*
- *How is your current service provider handling your...?*
- *What is your customer's feedback on the last project?*
- *What are the improvements you expect with the service that is currently offered?*
- *While looking for a new vendor what areas are given more priority?*
- *What areas you feel you are paying excess to your current service provider?*

Repercussion/ Impact Questions (Very Important!)

- *What happens when….?*
- *How much will that cost your organization?*
- *How big a problem will that be?*
- *Tell me…...*
- *Explain…….*
- *Describe…..*
- *What effect does that issue have on your xxxx dept?*
- *If this issue continues, what effects will that have on your……?*

Key for Solution Questions (Very important and leads you smoothly to the next step of the Sale ie; Proving Value)

- *What would it mean competitively, if you could just change or have……?*
- *How much better would the company image and your customer service be, if you could have...?*
- *By how much more would you be ahead of the competition if you had to….?*
- *If you had to do …., by how much would that save you?*

Remember: As a Sales Professional, there are 5 important **P's** in Selling. Your job is to first of all uncover the **Problems**, **Pains** and **Predicaments**, and only after which these could give rise to the **Possibilities** for you to **Prescribe**!...Till then, you as a telemarketer have no right to do so, and even if you do, this can drastically effect your credibility and future relationship. It is like a doctor trying to prescribe without diagnosing the case!

EXERCISE

Now keeping your customer in mind, look at building at least 5 questions each for 'Current Circumstances', 'Obstacles', 'Repercussions' and 'Key for Solution':

- Current Circumstances
- Obstacles
- Repercussions
- Key for Solution

What should the Sequential Pattern be in this stage?

1. A good way to begin is always start with Open Questions
   (Using either of the Questioning patterns mentioned above ie; Current, Desired, Barriers or Current Circumstances, Obstacles, Repercussions and Key for Solution)
2. Listen attentively
3. Take notes
4. Clarify/ Reconfirm with Closed Questions

A professional telemarketer ideally follows a sequential pattern at this stage, starting with Open Questions to uncover the Pain, Problems and their Repercussions and further follows it with Questions on the Key for Solutions.

While the customer talks, you as a professional would need to listen attentively.

'People were designed with two ears and one mouth, and that is the ratio in which to use them'!

How to be a good listener?

One of the greatest skills that you as a Sales Person can develop is the skill of listening. The best salespeople are the ones that do less talking and more of listening and that is why I believe God gave us two ears and one mouth- so we would do more listening than talking!

Here are some keys to be an "active" listener:

- Suspend judgment, initially- Keep an open mind
- Focus on the speaker and what he/she is saying
- Never interrupt while the customer speaks
- Tolerate silence. Silence can initially be uneasy, but if you practice tolerating it, you will find it very beneficial especially when negotiating.

- Listen for facts and key words
- Avoid distractions and never carry on side conversations
- Assess what you've heard
- Take notes of key points
- Clarify and reconfirm what the customer has told you- never assume!
- Never attempt doing anything else while on the phone with a customer! It's a big disturbance and bad manners

Before you respond, assess the information you heard by asking yourself four questions in your mind:
- *What has the customer told me?*
- *What can I do with this information?*
- *What else do I need to know?*
- *What questions do I still need to ask?*

To show you're listening actively:
- Respond by using terms like, *'Go on', Uh huh'* and *'mmm'*
- Stay always tuned in an alert

To show that you have, understood:
- Use, phrases like *"I see," "I understand"*
- Paraphrase, *"So you want me to ..."*

EXERCISE

What are areas that you would need to work on to improve your listening skills beginning from your very next call?

Taking Notes

A professional telemarketer will always takes notes of key points and never depend on memory.

As indicated in the 'Approach' step, you may like to indicate to the customer that you are taking notes: *"Is it okay Mr. Customer, if I jot down a few notes as we go along"*

By asking to take notes and doing so- even if the customer can't see you, you are subtly indicating to the customer:
- *I care about your business*
- *I do not want to miss anything*
- *The competition may have called you, but was more interested in the order- I am here to help!*
- *I am a professional*

Clarifying and Reconfirming with Closed Questions

This is the time when closed questions are very useful. To clarify and reconfirm, restate in your own words what the client has said and ask him to verify your understanding. An example would be: *'Mr Customer, Let me just take a minute to summarize, just to*

ensure that I've got the right information…You were mentioning that you were having a problem with….Am I right Mr. So & So?"
After the other person has confirmed your understanding, you have earned the right to proceed with additional questions to gain more information about the situation.

Why summarize regularly?
- *It keeps complexities under control*
- *It tests progress*
- *It lets you restate what the other party has said*
- *It can help gain the initiative*
- *It can keep the discussion on track*
- *It can prevent misinterpretation, misunderstanding and subsequent bitterness*
- *In other words, summarizing helps you stay on top (but you take the point).*

By summarizing, you are making sure you have the right information and that you haven't left out anything.

Proving Value of your Products/ Services

The Fourth Step in the Consultative Selling Process and another very important step is 'Proving the Value of your Product or Service' in the mind of the customer.

Usually the temptation for a telemarketer at this stage, once he/ she has identified the need is to immediately jump into recommending the solution- This can backfire with a number of objections, as the customer is yet not convinced on the value of your proposition. Therefore, there is one more step, before we actually get to recommend your solution; to build in the mind of the customer the value that your company and the product or service that matches the relevant need identified brings to them.
It is similar to what a good waiter would do in a restaurant. Before he takes your order he would literally make your mouth water by talking about the taste of the dishes by building up that appetite in you. So now when he does bring the dish to the table, you are ready to relish it!
Proving value is the process of showing your client how specific features of your product or service can offer benefits that will help your customer meet a business need, solve a problem or realize an opportunity that you had identified in the earlier step.
The purpose of Proving value is to demonstrate to the client the value of your product or service. Not all clients will be sure of the value; particularly new customers.
Proving value allows you to show the client why your product or service is an effective one and the value it brings to them, before you show the client how you can help them solve a problem/need or realize an opportunity with your recommendation.

Whenever people buy anything, there are two aspects that they are concerned about:
1. *What will the relevant product or service do for me/ my company- how will it help me? What value will we get from this?*
2. *Who or Which is the company behind this? Their standing? Will they support me when I need them? The Reliability factor!*

Let us look at the Product or Service first:
There are 3 aspects to any product or service. The **Features, Advantages** and **Benefits**
A Feature describes some *'characteristics'* of a product or service. Features are relatively neutral, both in their content and in their effect on the buyer. Features are those aspects of a product, or service that we can see, or describe. It is usually what the manufacturer or producer *'has put into'* the product.

Example:
  • *This mobile phone has a 'hands-free' facility*
When presenting features it is important to emphasize only those features that the customer said were most important (to the customer) during the probing phase of the sales process. These relate to the customers' buying criteria.

Now a number of telemarketers lose out big time because they just rattle 'only' the features of the product or service they are representing. And because of this the customer does not see the perceived value, because sometimes this could just sound technical and go over his head!

We need to translate each relevant feature into an ultimate 'Benefit' where he will be able to see value. In other words *what will it do* for the customer!

Again, some sales people make the mistake of mentioning all of the features of the product or service that they could think of during their presentation.

This is not helpful at all, but on the contrary confusing and can actually deter the customer from making a positive buying decision. It can indicate that the sales person wasn't listening effectively during the questioning phase of the sales process.

So as a professional telemarketer, it is for you now to translate this relevant Feature or Features that you just spoke of into an Advantage

An Advantage describes how a product, or a product feature, can be used or can help the buyer during the buying process.

Advantages, as you will see are more persuasive than features. ***Salespeople who talk about advantages sell more than salespeople who just feature dump.***

Building on the same example:

- *Because this mobile has a hand-free facility, you can use it safely to answer calls, while driving when the car is on the move*

At this stage, we need to remind ourselves that people buy because they have needs. If you as the seller can relate the product or service specifically to those needs identified in the earlier step, then there is a high probability of making a sale.

Benefits describe how the features and advantages will affect the buyer individually. They relate to the emotional buying behavior. In other words, the key is: ***what will the product or service do*** for them!

The key benefit words and statements are reassurance, confidence and peace of mind. Asking questions in the earlier stage was to identify needs. Once we have identified the buyers' main buying criteria we can link the appropriate Features to the relevant Advantages and Benefits.

Think **FAB!**

Going back now to our earlier example of the mobile phone…

- *Because our mobile has a hand-free facility you can be confident that if a customer calls you in the car, you can respond to the call quickly and safely and not miss out on vital enquiries or business opportunities, thus not losing out on your business.*

Every business has 5 main needs and your Benefit must address <u>one</u> or <u>more</u> of these …they are the **5** P's…

Profit- to make more money, that's why they are in business- savings, cost reductions etc

Protection- to ensure the security and safety of their business/ lives/ property etc,

Peace-A good night's sleep with no botheration or worry

Prestige-Wanting to stand out-Image! (for some!)

Performance- Improved productivity, more efficiency etc

In the example that we just covered, you will notice that the customer benefits by:
1. Business calls that could come in while he is driving: more revenue!
2. Safety while driving
3. To some- even prestigious using a 'hands-free' and driving

What is one phone call worth to him? If on an average he gets 10 business calls when driving, that could be the amount of business potential he could be missing out each day, if not attended to. So now the customer begins to see value in this feature of the product.

It is like an 'FM Radio Frequency' existing between the Buyer and Seller! **'WII-FM'**
It is like the customer always sending out signals of… **W**hat **I**s **I**n **I**t **F**or **M**e?
And until this Question is answered by the sales person, the Customer will never proceed!

What to keep in mind when working on solutions…
The customer's vision-short term/ long term
The customer's key challenges/ pains and requirements

Some examples might include:
- *Cost reduction;*
- *Improvement in quality;*
- *Improvement in end – user satisfaction;*
- *Regulatory or legislation changes;*
- *Capacity increase;*
- *Innovation;*
- *Reduction of customer's 'churn' (customers' moving away);*
- *Increase in diversity of offering (adding new products or services);*
- *Replacement of previous or incumbent supplier*

<u>**EXERCISE**</u>
List all the relevant features of your product / service. Then translate each of the respective features into an Advantage and a Benefit.
REMEMBER: The relevant benefit must address the Question: *"What's in it for the Customer?"* And must address 1 or more of the 5 P's seen above.

<u>Features</u>   <u>Advantages</u>   <u>Benefits</u>

As mentioned, the other aspect of Proving Value has to do with the company that is backing the relevant product or service.
When Proving Value of your Company, it is important to keep in mind the USP's of your company– or 'Unique Selling Propositions'…*What is it that makes your company stand out from the others. What is so special about your company? Why should the customer move from his current vendor to deal with your company?*
Your USP's have to be strong enough for it to draw the customer to you!

Few pointers are suggested below that can help you think further:
- *Stability of Company/ Expertise*
- *Years of Standing*
- *Special Service Features/ Capabilities*
- *Terms and Conditions*
- *Creativity*
- *Alliances and Partnerships*
- *Leveraging outside resources and partners network to service our clients*
- *Awards/ Recognitions*

<u>EXERCISE</u>
Try listing as many USP's that you can think of that differentiates your company from the competition

Standing out and differentiating from the competition!

This is a very interesting and powerful 'Exercise' you could undertake every time you are about to make a call to a major customer, or to a large/ key account and can be done well ahead of your call equipping you well enough on of how to deal with the competition, should the customer raise or compare the two.

As we have seen above, people make decisions based on what the product or service will do for them, along with the company backing this.

Keeping the Product/ Service and the company backing it, we can now say that customers would be ideally seeking **Value** on one hand and **Uniqueness** on the other.

So list all features of your offering that you think makes you **Unique** (from the customers' angle or perception) and the perceived **Value** to the Customer (ideally about 10 to 15)

S. No.	Feature	Uniqueness	Value
1.	Example 1	8	9

Rate **Uniqueness** and **Value** respectively (on a 0 to 10 scale based on how you feel the customer perceives it) From client to client it will differ.

Remember: What can be relevant for one client can be irrelevant for other clients!

Now plot them on a Quadrant with **Value** on **x axis** and **Uniqueness** on the other **y axis**

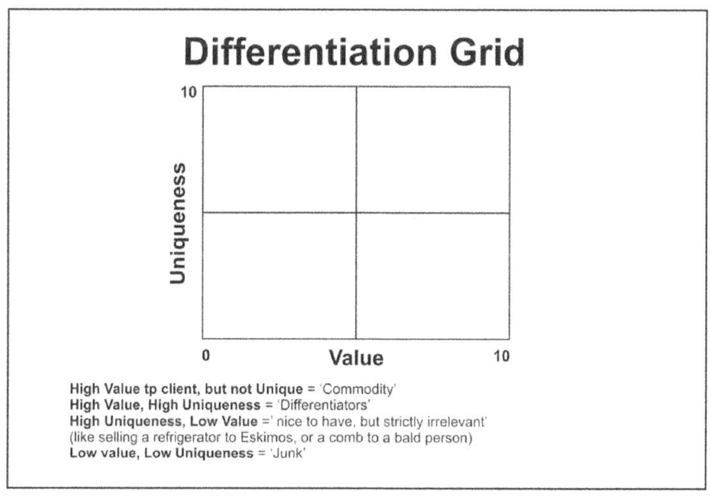

Once you've plotted these features on to the 4 quadrants, we now need to see what is of relevance, so we could use only those features that matter to the client, based on the need identified…

When its **High on Value** and **High on Uniqueness**- then these are your **key 'Differentiators'** (The ones appearing in the top right hand corner quadrant)
The features that are in this quadrant are the ones that <u>only you</u> are offering. These are your differentiators. If done really well, then this could indicate that this is what makes you stand out!

High on Value to the client, but **not Unique**, is a **'Commodity'** (the bottom right quadrant)
Any feature appearing in this quadrant is what your competition is also offering- just like you! Nothing great! When you start talking these features, you are on the same battle ground as your competition. The customer now compares you with others.

High Uniqueness and **Low in Value** could be 'nice to have, but strictly irrelevant' to the customer (Top left hand corner) – It does not make sense at all to the customer. The need and the relevant features are a mismatch (like trying to sell a fridge to Eskimos or a comb to a bald person!)

When it is **Low in Value** and **Low in Uniqueness**, just discard these as 'Junk'(Bottom left quadrant)-Don't even look at them or talk of them!

Caution: To be done in your office away from the customer before your call, and never to be given to the customer

Handling Customer Concerns and Objections

An important component at this stage (or can happen earlier too) is: The Handling of Objections.

During the Sales Process, even the best salespeople can encounter objections that are difficult to handle. An objection is a concern or question raised by the client that delays or prevents you from proceeding to the next step in the Consultative Selling Cycle.

By using the right techniques, however, you can handle these objections without losing your focus.

Whenever I come to this part I am always reminded of why farmers place a 'scare-crow' in the middle of a paddy or rice field. The answer is obvious- to scare away the birds. But a clever bird knows that behind this so called 'scare-crow' are juicy grains- or his food!

So also, I believe, that a smart telemarketer knows that behind every objection there is a genuine need to buy! The objection in question must however be handled or cleared before progress is made.

Why do you think customers raise objections?
During the sales process customers will raise objections for many reasons. At some stage, customers could:

- *Misunderstand something you have said.*
- *Feel pressurized.*
- *Are not convinced about your claims.*
- *Haven't yet made up their mind.*
- *Have to go back and justify their buying decision to others.*

One of the most common times objections are raised is just <u>before</u> the decision to purchase. In this case the customer is often looking for reassurance that the decision to buy is the right one.

We must understand however, that objections form a natural part of the buying process. Just before making a buying decision the buyer worries about making a mistake. And we all do this every day, even for the smallest purchase, so why get worked up when the customer does so?

So if an objection is raised at this stage, it means that the buyer has an unanswered question or concern that the salesperson has to deal with and it could most times be a positive rather than a negative situation when a customer raises an objection

Mostly, there are basically **two types** of objections that you will encounter:
Doubt
Indifference

Doubt, sometimes is referred to as distrust, and is expressed when the client doesn't believe something you have said.

Indifference on the other hand is expressed when the client feels that what you have said is not important to him – the client may simply feel that it is not appropriate to their situation.
Both types of objections occur for specific reasons. To overcome an objection, you need to recognize why it occurred and then deal with it, **immediately.**

Clarifying Objections
Clarify what the objection is (express empathy if appropriate)
Then respond accordingly:
- To remove doubt:
    - *Refer to a similar situation and/or*
    - *Offer evidence or proof that what you have said is true*

- To handle indifference:
    - *If based on a misunderstanding or lack of information, explain your point more thoroughly and or*
    - *Outweigh the indifference with the benefits of your suggested approach*

Now we need to deal with the objection: Once you fully understand the nature of the objection then it can be answered in different ways depending on whether it is
- a misunderstanding by the customer
- disbelief over claims you are making
- a product disadvantage.

You will now need to verify that the objection is removed or cleared from the mind of the customer and to ensure it does not come up later.
Your next step would be to 'advance the sale'.
The key to objection handling is to react less quickly when an objection is raised and find out more about the problem. Clarify exactly what the problem is; then try to overcome the objection.
Finally, if you have dealt with the objection successfully and it is the right time, close the sale, or move on to the next stage of the sales process.

<u>EXERCISE</u>
Before we go any further, list down all the possible objections you have come across so far or you come across regularly (Whatever comes to your mind):
We would get to dealing with them as we move forward.

Most objections or customer concerns can broadly be classified under **4 key heads**, as you will see in the illustration.

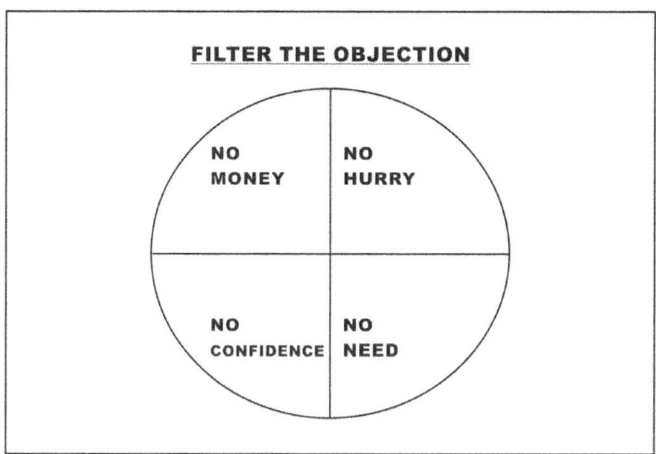

Now try to classify under which quadrant each of your objections (you listed above in the Exercise) fall in under:
For example; If a customer says: *'Your rates are too high'* or *'You guys are very costly'*
Obviously this would feature under the quadrant '**NO MONEY'**
Another example for 'NO MONEY': *'I need a discount!'*

'I don't want to deal with your company again. I had a bad experience last year'!
Or *'Never heard of your company…not too sure about them'!*
Examples like the two above will fall in under the '**NO CONFIDENCE'** Quadrant.

An example of what would come under the quadrant of '**NO HURRY'** would be something like this: *'I am fairly happy with what we have now. We could possibly look at this later only'*
Or *'I don't need any changes right now'* or *'We have enough of this for now'*

The last quadrant '**NO NEED'** is a little tricky and could be something like this: We are n*ot interested'* or *'Please don't call me again'* or *'I don't need you guys'*

Now once you have classified all your objections under the four respective quadrants, let us see what each means and how to go about handling them.

NO MONEY
Do you think the Customer really does not have that additional money?
What he is actually conveying to you by raising that concern that falls in this quadrant is that he does not really see value in your proposition. And most times it will be that the telemarketer has been rattling off features of his/her product or service, without really proving value of how the customer will benefit or what it would do for him.

TIP: Keep 'FAB' in mind. Prove value by translating the relevant features to benefits. What is in it for the customer? What will it do for him- translate into tangible benefits that he can see, that far outweighs what he would be investing in.

NO CONFIDENCE
There could be 2 scenarios here:
1. A past customer who has had bad experience and now no more wants to deal with you
2. A new customer who has never heard of you and doubts your company's capability

If it is a past customer, how would we go about building his confidence again in your company and service?

TIP: Talk to them and email them testimonials of satisfied customers in the same business as theirs, pictures/ videos or arrange site visits to such customers, case stories of how you resolved similar cases and the outcome, have them connect on phone right away with such customers who will talk well of you etc. You could also build on the USP's of your company, particularly relevant to his company and need

If it is a new customer, who has never heard of your company and doubts its capability, then how would we go about instilling and building his confidence in your company and service?

TIP: This is where the USP's prepared under the step Proving Value will help. You could highlight the USP's of your company particularly relevant to his company and need. Send them testimonials/ video clips of satisfied customers in the same business as theirs, site visits to such customers etc. Particularly of interest would be your credibility, standing in the market, your after-sales-support and financial status.

NO HURRY
How do we get the customer to take or commit on a decision now?
TIP: Look at what incentives you have now that the customer could benefit by.
What if your company does not have the required material when he requires?
With the costs of raw materials, labour etc going up, what is the guarantee that he would get your product/ services at this same rate?

NO NEED
Any objection falling in this quadrant is probably one of the most difficult. There are 2 possibilities:
1. There is genuinely no need- He may not be a likely customer
2. He has a need but has not disclosed

If it is the second scenario, then we will need to go back to step 3 of the Selling Skills plan which is Fact-finding or Probing to uncover further. If the customer is still unwilling to reveal, then in most times it could be something personal about you as an individual that he is put off with.
TIP: Allow a few days for him to cool down, and then have someone senior from your organization call them to build up again

Here are some of the most common objections telemarketers face, along with suggested responses:

"The economy is terrible right now after this pandemic, and business is really bad. I can't spend any money now."
Possible solution: *"Your competitors are going through the same tough times as you are, but if you have to stay above them, then I have some specific plans that will help increase your sales and make your business stronger. This will make sure your business is on top as the economy improves."*

"I have to check with my partner."
 Possible solution: *"Why not speak with them right now and get that okay so we can go forward right away on this?* Or *"Could we get them on a conference call with us now if it is okay with you, so we would be able to move forward on this"*

"Let me think it over."
Possible solution: *"I understand that you don't want to make a hasty decision. Mr. Customer, tell me, what exactly is it that you want to think about?"*
If someone abruptly states, *"I'm not interested"* politely ask, *"What is it you are not interested in?"* Use the answer to keep him or her on the phone and continue and get back to the next step.

"Send me some more information,"
Respond by asking, *"What type of information can I provide you with that will help you make an informed decision?"*
Or
"OK! Then when I send you the information, how long will you need to make a decision?"
And after they answer, you can already set up a fixed date to call back.
Better, you can add *"But I don't want to waste your time, so before I send you the information, I need to ask you just a couple of quick questions."*

"I'm busy and can't talk right now,"
Ask when would be a better time for you to call back. Try to set a fixed appointment, then, quickly go back to restating the benefit you're offering.

Handling the PRICE Objection
Price is probably one of the most common objections we hear in sales. Customers will say *'you are too expensive'*, but before we react, we need to think about what it might mean when they say so.
Sadly, most sales people respond immediately with a *'No Sir….'* rather than trying to understand what was in the customers mind when he said this!

You need to put yourself in the clients shoes!
Perceptions Differ! We need to specifically understand…
How short is short!
How firm is firm!
How slim is slim!

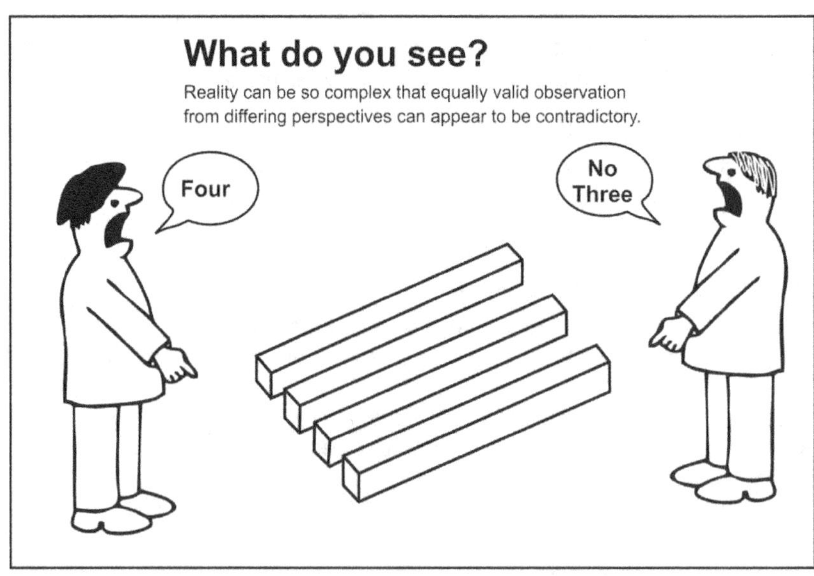

As seen from the 2 illustrations above, perceptions of individuals differ. So all the more it makes sense to clarify the customers understanding of *'prices are high'* or *'too expensive'* before we hastily jump into handling the same

Too expensive could mean several of these and more:

- *I've had another quote*
- *I'm checking you out*
- *I'm negotiating with you*
- *I have to go back and convince others*
- *It's more than I expected*
- *It's more than I have in my budget*
- *I don't want to buy from you*

This is why it is so important to clarify this objection before we attempt to handle it. We need to find out the real reasons behind the objection. Often we react too quickly and give what we feel is the right answer, but in fact we could be totally wrong.

The customer may have had another quote and may have constituents to satisfy. They may be looking for help etc. Interrupting or not clarifying but giving an inappropriate answer will not help the customer achieve their buying objectives.

Steps to handling an Objection

One of the best ways to answer any sales objection is to:

1. **Listen to the objection:** Resist the temptation of interrupting the customer. You may have heard the objection a hundred times but not from this particular customer. It may also be that the customer has more than one objection, or that this particular objection is slightly different than the ones you usually hear.
2. **Prevent further objections arising:** Actually one great way to ensure that this objection never surfaces again or another one does not come up again after you've handled the first one is to ask a question that could go something like this: *'Mr Customer, before I go into answering this concern for you…let me clarify…Is this the only concern that is preventing you from moving forward?"* In most case the customer will say *'Oh, Yes'*. Now what you've actually done is to indirectly prevent him from coming up with any further excuses in the future!
3. **Filter the Objection**: See which of the 4 quadrants of NO MONEY, NO HURRY, NO CONFIDENCE, NO NEED (covered above) it falls into
4. **If Price, clarify the objection:** To clarify the objection you could say something like: *"When you say we are expensive, could you be a little more specific, Mr. Customer?"* Listen to what the customer says. He would then clarify why he feels you are expensive. Based on his answer you could move forward. If he is comparing you with the competition, then use your differentiation grid (covered earlier) to stand out.

In closing this chapter I'd like to use a quote that I stumbled upon, that is called I believe **"The Common Law of Business Balance"** which is a meditation on price and is attributed to **John Ruskin** – a 19th century English poet, fervent art critic, and socialist.

'There is hardly anything in the world that some man cannot make a little worse and sell a little cheaper. People who consider price only are this man's lawful prey.

It's unwise to pay too much, but it's unwise to pay too little.

When you pay too much you lose a little money; that is all.

When you pay too little, you sometimes lose everything, because the thing you bought was incapable of doing the thing you bought it to do.

The common law of business balance prohibits paying a little and getting a lot. It can't be done.

If you deal with the lowest bidder, it's well to add something for the risk you run.

And if you do that, you will have enough to pay for something better.

Presenting your Recommendation/ Solution

We are now at the Fifth Step of the Selling Process, which is the Recommendation Stage
Actually, if you have brought the customer right up to here, you will realize that this particular step is a mere formality of wrapping up the entire discussion.

Recommending may follow Proving Value with some customers (for example to new customers) or can happen immediately after Fact-Finding with other clients that have already dealt with your company (who are familiar with the features and benefits you have to offer)
The purpose of Recommending is to show the client the specific product features and benefits which will solve their needs / problems. It is the process of presenting your specific product or service solution to fulfill one or more needs identified during Fact Finding

Steps
- Summarize the client's needs(s)/problem(s)
- Recap the Value from your product/ service related to the need(s)/problem(s)
- Recommend the appropriate Solution

Closing the Sale

Closing is the **Sixth** and **Final Step** in the Consultative Selling Cycle.
It is the focal point of the cycle and it involves obtaining the client's commitment to take a suggested action.
The purpose of this step is to obtain the client's commitment to take the action that you have suggested or recommended.
In fact, if you've done till here, following all the steps outlined so far, you will invariably find the customer ready and already agreeing with you!

So what then prevents telemarketers from closing?
Many sales people are looking for 'closing techniques' that will make the decision making process easier and take away some of the pressure felt by both buyer and seller at that moment of truth, when a decision is about to be made.
The problem is that at this point the telemarketer is worried about getting rejected and how he/she will have to face the boss, whilst the buyer is worried about making a mistake. So it is all too easy for either or both sides to delay the buying decision, rather than risking rejection, or taking the wrong decision
It is up to you as the telemarketer to have the confidence, at the right time, to ask for a commitment and risk rejection. That is your role and unfortunately, 7 times out of 10 telemarketers fail to ask for some kind of commitment and this can make them lose the sale they have been working on so hard to achieve- by allowing the competition to come in at this stage. All their hard work is eaten up by the competition. .
Research has shown that 70% of sales contacts end up with the salesperson not asking for a commitment, or an order as the case maybe. Fear of rejection takes over and we miss the opportunity to close. While many sales people see closing as being about techniques this is not actually the main issue.

Closing is about **timing** rather than **techniques**.

So what then is 'Closing'?
The sales process is about seeking out problems and trying to identify solutions. We cannot close the customer, or gain some sort of commitment from them until there is an identified need for our solution.
It used to be said in the earlier days '**ABC of Selling**'- meaning to "**A**lways **b**e **c**losing" but this approach does not fit in with relationship selling. The right time to close is when the customer is ready to buy. If the telemarketer is always trying to close this will irritate most customers and they will probably reject the salesperson- this is also one of the reasons why this is the most hated profession as seen earlier. So closing is about timing, not technique. The best way to sell is to make it easy for the customer to buy. The close is important and we should have the confidence to ask for the order at the appropriate time. However, we must put the close into perspective and keep selling simple.

A few Important Points about Closing

Closing the sale is an integral part of the sales process:
Before a buyer will place an order with you, he or she will have to see a need for your product and be convinced that your particular product represents the best solution to the problem represented by that need.

No salesperson ever closed every sale:
Everyone who has ever sold professionally has had to get used to living with rejection. A good salesperson will always be rejected more times than he or she is successful. Every time you fail, you move closer to the time you will succeed.

Selling is a 'numbers game':
Given a 'basic' level of skill in sales techniques, the amount you sell is directly related to the number of calls you make. The more customers you see, the more business you will close.

Certain key ratios apply to your sales activity:
By measuring your sales performance over a period of time you will understand more fully the key ratios that apply to your business

The right time to close is when the customer is ready to buy:
This is so important. Closing tends to happen towards the end of the sales call but don't assume this will always be the case. If the customer wants to buy early into your sales presentation then you should get a commitment straight away.

Look for more than one opportunity to close the sale:
There will be several occasions during the sale when the customer is ready to buy. There will also be more than one opportunity for you to close the sale.

Buyer resistance is natural and should be expected:
Often when the buyer hesitates during the closing stages he or she is seeking reassurance from the salesperson in a consultative, non-threatening way, that the decision that is about to be made, is a good decision.

Buyers seldom ask you for the order:
Most buyers rely on the telemarketer to make the buying process easy for them. However, they rarely ask for the order outright, so the most effective and most obvious closing technique, having gone through the several stages of the call, is to ask the buyer if he or she wishes to place an order.

Some suggestions to help you Close

The easiest and most effective close is to:
Ask for the order It has been estimated that 7 out of every 10 sales contacts end without the salesperson asking for the order, or some form of commitment. This is due either to lack of confidence, or fear of rejection.

The Assumptive close uses a question that is phrased in a way that assumes the customer is going ahead with the sale. Eg: *When/Where will you want delivery?*

The Alternative close gives a choice between two positive alternatives. Closing on a small issue is about choosing a minor feature of your product or service and gaining agreement from the buyer on that feature. Eg: *Will you prefer us to start Tue or Wed?*

The Pressure close enables you to put pressure on the buyer in terms of special offers or inducements that are available or penalties for not placing the order. Eg: *This price is only available up to the end of this month.*

Converting on objections: An objection can be a very strong buying signal. If the buyer raises an objection and it is the only objection that is preventing the order from being placed you can use this to gain commitment to buy.

Eg: *You have said Mr. Buyer that you are interested in our services, but the schedule that we are talking of is unacceptable to you. Is this the only concern you have? If we are able to work out a compromise would you be willing to place an order today?*

The Negotiated close: Standard negotiating techniques are very useful at the closing stages of the sales process.

Eg: If *I am able to reduce my price by 10% will you agree today?* (can be used for delivery also!)

If you have to give a reduction in price, always try to make it sound difficult and get something back in return

Eg: The customer says: "*Give me 10% discount and we have a deal*"

- The temptation, as a salesperson is to agree and secure the sale. A good negotiator would react differently and try to win a concession.
- "*This is extremely difficult, but if I am able to look at our discount structure, and if we were to go down that route I would then need a 2 year contract. Would that be possible?*"
- If the customer agrees two year contract is possible, then we can offer 10%, or perhaps less

The Trial or Test close is used during your presentation and gets feedback from the customer on what they have heard so far.

 Eg: Listen to what the buyer says, summarize what has been said and ask for the order/ close the sale

Do you have all the information on which to make a decision?

The Choice close: Gives two or more alternatives. Eg: *"May I send you an email of the order we have discussed or would you prefer sending me a confirmation by tomorrow?"*

Finally, the **balance sheet method** is used where you are in direct competition with another company. List all the points in favor of your product and all the points against on sheet of paper.

This is repeated for the competitor product. If your product is the stronger of the alternatives available to the buyer this method can help the final decision be made in your favor.

After asking for the order, just **shut up!** (I have seen many sales personnel messing up at this stage by opening their mouths on something irrelevant and allowing the customer to go off on a tangent- thereby delaying or postponing and sometimes even losing the sale all together!)

Finally, the experience of bagging an order, whatever be the size usually gives every sales person a joyous feeling and the word **'SALE'** says it all:

S - Such

A - A

L - Lovely

E - Experience!

At-a-Glance-Summary of the 6 Step Selling Plan

- **Preparation**

Self- Mental/ Physical
Client Info (including Creditworthiness)
 Market/ Industry/ Competition
 Sales Tools
 Your Strategy

- **Approach**

Salutation
Self
Company/Product
Convenient time
Purpose of call
Qualify for Authority: (Use: WANTS, FAINT or BANT)
Interest Creating Remark
Permission to move to next step

- **Fact-Finding (Uncovering Needs)**

(Use General Questions / Specific Questions/ Get customers' participation)
The step should identify the customer's
- Current Situation
- Desired Situation
- Existing Barriers

Questions to unravel: Pain, Problems & Predicaments.
Use the C.O.R.K. Model
Questions on:
- Market
- Competition(current supplier/rates)
- His future /long term plans

Listen and Take Notes
Paraphrase with Closed Questions

- **Proving Value**

Talk of your service
Link the features to the benefit and what's in it for them (sell Benefits!)
Relate Benefits to needs identified through Fact finding
Use visual descriptions/ Create a movie in customers mind
Create desire

- **Recommendation**

Provide the product as a solution to the need that has been identified.
Answer customer concerns/ Handle Objections
Clear all doubts
- **Close-by asking for the order or obtaining a commitment!**

Handling turn downs/ rejections and keeping yourself motivated

After a series of calls where you don't achieve your objectives, it is quite natural to face call reluctance, sulk and withdraw. I have seen many telemarketers, who would gladly do anything but pick up the phone again and dial or hit the button for the next customer. This is normal. It happens when you take the rejection personally. Whatever happens, you cannot take rejection to heart- as even the rudest customers are actually not rejecting you personally. Fear of rejection is real and common. Recognize it and let it go.

Here are some ways to get yourself up and back again
- Take a few moments to meditate and clear your mind after a particularly difficult or frustrating call.
- Talk to a colleague about how you are feeling, and remember to be supportive to colleagues when they talk to you too.
- Understand sales ratios: You should have a good idea of what the average closing ratio is in your industry so you can have realistic expectations. For example if you are aware that with every 1 in 25 calls usually results in a sale, it ensures that you set the right expectations by which to measure your success.
- Set your mind to remove the roadblocks that are holding you back from developing and maintaining the attitude you need to achieve success.
- Instead of focusing on the negatives of rejection, it's important to think about how you can create positives from the situation. What did you learn from the whole situation? As well as helping to improve your mindset and make the working day even better, this positive attitude will be reflected in your success rate and could help you achieve more than you ever thought possible.
- Remember that competency and confidence are two key elements that allow salespeople to achieve success. If you have both, other obstacles can be overcome easily.
- Focus on solutions, not on problems- So concentrate on achieving success as opposed to worrying about failure.
- Keep reminding yourself of previous successes, and reward yourself even for reaching smaller goals.
- Before picking up the phone, envision yourself achieving success and closing sales. Focus on how you felt the last time you made a great and successful sale and recapture that feeling as you embark on making new calls.
- Visualize yourself succeeding: the customer appreciating you-your boss and colleagues applauding your efforts.
- Use positive self talk. It's garbage in: garbage out. If you feed your brain negative stuff, it affects your approach, your tone, your language and how you come across. So, practice positive self-talk (especially after rejection) and you'll experience less rejection in the first place.

- Encourage yourself to remember the last time you had a really good call just before making a fresh call. This will help to fuel enthusiasm when you make a call
- If you are a manager or supervisor of a telemarketing team, develop a daily or weekly reward system or method of recognition for your top achievers. Give people something to work towards and motivate them with a friendly competition.
- Keep rewarding yourself for the successes you achieve in order to stay motivated and focused.
- Listen to talks of motivational speakers or read something that you find motivational.
- Try to surround yourself with positive people only who inspire and support you.
- Listen to upbeat music. This will help motivate you and keep you pepped up.
- Reinforce in your mind that by making sales, you're not just helping yourself and your company; you're also helping your customers, because what you're offering can benefit them or will help them solve a problem.
- Everyone has their own goals that motivate them. It's important to determine what yours are early on and stay focused on them. Review your personal goals and objectives and focus on why you developed these goals. Make sure the goals you have are attainable. If, for example, you're saving money for a dream house or your marriage, picture that objective in your mind.
- Share success stories and be able to humorously look at the negative aspects of your job or situation in order to work through them and move on.

REMEMBER: Sales is a people business and people buy people. Therefore, if you can maintain your positive attitude and apply some of these principles, not only will you be better placed to handle rejection, you'll experience less rejection in the first place and stay on top always!.

Post- Mortem: Evaluating your Call

Evaluating your own Call

As a Professional it is of key importance that you build a system of Self-Coaching, to help you keep constantly working on your Competencies and Performance. It is based on the principle of: *'What I say to myself, is more important than what others say to me'* You could, after every major call use the format shown below to evaluate the steps of your sales call. Keep doing this on a regular basis to ensure the bar moves from left to right for each specific step or area of your call

Role Play- Observation Sheet:

Name: ___________________

FACTS	EVALUATION on STANDARDS			COMMENTS
Steps	Good	Average	Poor	Specially what I saw/heard

Preparation
-Mental/Self Image
-Account:
    -Client (including Credit)
    -Market/Industry/ Competition
    -Sales Tools
    -Strategy (Questions/Concerns)
Approach
-Introduction-Salutation
    -Self/Company
    -Convenient Time
    -ICR
    -Permission to move
Fact Finding
-Builds Rapport
-Checks Decision Maker
Questions
-Current
-Desired
-Barriers
or
(...to uncover Pain Areas/ Problems)
    -Circumstances/ Current
    -Obstacles/ Problems
    -Repercussions/ Implications
    -Key for Solutions
-Listening Skills
-Note Taking
-Summarizes with Closed Questions
Proving Value
-USP of Company
-FAB of Product
-Uses Differentiation Grid
-Handles Objections/Concerns
-Recognizes client agreement
Recommends & Closes
-Summarizes Need/ Problem identified
-Recommends Appropriate Solution
-Shows how business needs will be met
-Thanks Customer
Professional Demeanor
Attitude
Assertive/ Confidence
Tone of voice
Volume of voice
Use of language
Posture
Other Comments

Role-playing a sales call

The more you practice, the more you become an expert and a professional. So here are ways that you can practice role-playing at least twice a week. Keep doing this regularly and note what it does to your confidence and performance!

1. Work in teams of three or more to prepare for a role playing situation in which one will be the customer and the other the telemarketer and the rest as observers.

2. A short script of the sales call should be prepared in which the telemarketer is to have one of the following scenarios as the call objective:

a. Introduce the customer to the company and the line of products available for sale and complete a sale for a single product line

b. Explain a new product available on the market from the telemarketing firm.

c. Explain a new sales promotion campaign being made available to the customer business.

d. Any others that may be developed by your Supervisor

3. Participants may use telephone equipment if available. If none is available, participants may role play their telephone conversation while sitting back to back so that they will not see each other, or they can be separated by a partition

4. Other members in the group may be observers and should critique the sales call by providing feedback on the positives, the areas of improvement- particularly in the steps of the sale, the voice (confidence, modulation etc), any distracting mannerisms displayed by the telemarketer etc. Use the Evaluation Sheet provided earlier.

5. Each team should have the opportunity to role play their telephone conversation.

6. Recording the telephone conversations may be useful for assessing participant progress.

Some other 'Role Playing Situations'
1. Late delivery of a product, causing the loss of customers.
2. Defective product, creating need to return to company.
3. Service personnel not solving problem on installed equipment.
4. Overcharge on account resulting in inaccurate billing.
5. Assessment of late charges on bill already paid.

Additional situations can be developed for role playing.

Key Factors for a Tele-marketer to enable you stand out

- Always tell the truth! Be honest -it really is the best approach. You WILL get found out if you lie. If you do not know something admit it with the assurance that you would get back with the answer. And do so as committed! Using methods that are honest and forthright is what separates a professional from the rest.
- Wear some armor- Telemarketing isn't easy. You need to build some resilience to rejection. If you don't, it will be a task that becomes increasingly scary. It isn't for the faint hearted. Constantly find ways to keep yourself charged up.
- Your attitude determines your altitude! Always have a positive attitude.
- Begin each shift with a positive attitude and try your best to maintain that attitude throughout the day – even if you get discouraged. Prospects will notice a negative tone in your voice. A positive and upbeat tone, however, can be contagious
- Smile-It transmits to your voice. Your customer can actually feel it
- Telephone during "up" time - Best times are 9 AM to Noon; 2 PM to 4 PM; Never on Monday mornings or Friday afternoons. Never on Sundays or holidays.
- Block Your Time - Make or return phone calls at precisely the exact time you committed to. Don't even be 2-3 minutes late!
- Don't dwell on small talk: Small talk at the beginning of each call might seem friendly and natural. But too much of it can be distracting and time wasting.
- Predetermine how to maximize the value of every call. Before you speak to a prospect, have a game plan for all possibilities… if plan "A" doesn't work, you should be able to roll to plan "B" and "C" if necessary.
- Always follow-up! Never give up. If the customer fails to call back, never assume they are not interested. They could be just caught up with other things. Persistence matters from your end!
- Be Diligent: You want to make sure that each day is better than the previous day, in terms of number of calls, quality of calls, your updating of call register etc
- Build relationships and use your existing customers to provide you references. These are powerful!
- Always be fully prepared: An outline for your script, the probing questions, possible answers to objections etc
- Use frames of reference -Past work, client reference points, and industry examples
- Learn as much as you can about your customer like practices, other customers in that business, trends in that business- so you could talk with authority
- Always keep records of every call, even of the minutest conversations
- Don't try to be different on phone from the person you would be In person: The other person should feel as if you were face to face and talking. So be natural. Be yourself. Let your phone presence be a reflection of your live presence

- Listen more than you talk!
- Role-play or record your calls to see what could have been done better. Listen back to improve your techniques. Make a record of what you've learnt from every call and improvise as you go forward.

Some important lessons in Tele-marketing
10 Mistakes to avoid!

1. **Never ask:** *'How are you are today'* or *'how is business?'* - It is a tell-tale sign of a typical sales call, and you are asking for trouble!
2. **Getting distracted by ANYTHING else whilst on a call:** i.e. text messages, emails, colleagues, Facebook! Don't have your mobile on when making calls, you will be tempted to look to see who is calling and this will tell the prospect your attention is not 100% on them
3. **Using the wrong tone of voice:** Because the person to whom you are speaking cannot see you, the telephone focuses full attention on the tone of your voice. Make a recording of your voice. Then listen to it. What kind of image do you get of yourself? Is this how you would want to project yourself to others? Let someone else hear the recording.
4. **Improper rate of speech:** The telephone exaggerates your rate of speech. If you speak too rapidly, it is hard for the other person to understand what you are saying. This, in turn, can lead to mistrust. On the other hand, speaking too slowly can lead to impatience or may sound boring to the listener. The average rate of speech is 150 words per minute. Find a 750 word article or speech. Read it aloud as you time yourself. You should read the message in exactly five minutes. Continue to practice until you can do it consistently, without fluctuating more than 10% either way.
5. **Not getting to the right decision maker:** Too often salesmen are willing to settle on the phone for the "assistant manager" instead of the real buying authority or the key decision maker. You are better off finding out when he will be back than wasting this selling opportunity with a non-decision maker.
6. **Failure to check on the decision makers' availability to talk**: Good courtesy and good business suggests you clear the way before getting deep into the call. If he is in the middle of something, it is better to know and call back, rather than disturb and destroy a sale.
7. **Not offering the buyer a compelling reason to listen**: When you first call a stranger, you face built-in resistance. He does not know you. He might not know your company. He does not know much about what you have to offer, and he cannot see what you look like. You have to offer him a reason for listening -- a benefit. Do not merely ask for his time. It is precious. Instead, offer him something in return. It is pretty difficult to turn down a benefit.
8. **Not uncovering the needs of the customer**: Failure to listen is probably the single, biggest failure of salesmen. Remedy: plan your phone calls in advance. What questions are you going to ask? Be ready to adapt your presentation to the customer's needs. That will take some research on your part.
9. **Assuming you understood the buyer correctly:** Understanding exactly what the buyer is saying is essential to your being able to serve him properly. Therefore, you must keep an accurate record of what is said. Take notes. Read

back details to the buyer, before you continue. This feedback assures the buyer that you understood him correctly.

10. **Assuming that the buyer heard you correctly**: It is necessary to get reassurance from the buyer that he understands what you are saying. Use test questions such as – "How would this relate to your situation?" Interject test questions frequently to determine if you and he are really heading toward a sale

Taking this forward!

What's the next step?
As a Professional Telemarketer, you would constantly need to remind yourself that Training is like Hygiene! Just as how you would need to have a shower every day in order to stay fresh, so also you would need to keep yourself abreast and updated by constantly working on your skill sets and upgrading them from time to time. Just reading a book from cover to cover will not guarantee a change in the way you work. No idea or concept is worth anything, if it cannot be applied to real situations. So applying these principles by putting them to immediate practice is the KEY!

So how do you do that?
Well here are a few tips to help you do so…
- Set time to practice with Role-Plays!
- Maybe an hour a week- You could do it with your colleagues or someone you trust.
- Work on perfecting one step at a time! Don't aim to excel in all steps. One step at a time!
- Do periodic evaluation of your skills. See where you are today. Set a benchmark or standard to reach say in 3 months. Evaluate to see if you've moved in that direction.
- Keep this as a regular routine- Practice consistency!
- Read at least one book on 'Skill Development' a month and observe/ study Top Performers! There are many books…today even free pdf books that one could download.
- Remember my favorite saying, (I used it at the start of this book!): *"If you continue to do what you are always doing, you will continue to get what you are always getting"*
- In other words if we want something better than what we have today, we need to change our current style of working.

I do hope you've enjoyed and benefitted from this book. I thank you for your time and your desire to develop.

Should you have any Questions or any Suggestions that you'd want us to cover in a forthcoming book that can help you as well as others, feel free to write to: training@SalesTrainingIndia.com

We wish you all Success as an Eagle Seller!

Gerard Assey

About the Author

Gerard Assey is a Graduate in Economics, a PGD in Management (HRD) and holds a Doctorate in Leadership. Gerard holds several International Qualifications in Sales, Debt Collection, Training & Teaching, and is a 'Fellow' of the prestigious 'Institute of Sales & Marketing Management'-UK, a Certified NLP Practitioner, a 'Certified Trainer', an 'Accredited Management Teacher-Behavioral Sciences', a 'Certified Competency Facilitator' and a 'Certified Management Consultant'- (the International credentials of a professional management consultant, awarded in accordance with global standards of the ICMCI); He is also a Member of the 'National Association of Sales Professionals' & a Member of the 'Institute of Management Consultants' backed with several years experience in varied industries, both in India and Overseas. He also holds an 'Etiquette Consultant' Certification from the USA (by Sue Fox, Author of Best Seller: 'Business Etiquette for Dummies'. She has trained some of the top celebrities' world over). He was also a recipient of a scholarship for extensive training in Japan on 'Corporate Management for India'.

Gerard Assey is 'Founder & Chief Corporate Trainer' of the Group: '**Citius, Altius, Fortius Unlimited'**- an organization that **celebrated 19 years of Glorious Service** in **2020**, focusing on 3 Core Competencies: People. Performance. Profit; in functional areas of Sales & Marketing, HR & Organizational Development, covering Recruitment, Training & Consultancy!

Gerard was instrumental in setting up and building one of the very 1st few professional telesales team in India from a 3 member team to over 300 members, and having managed organizations with large Sales Forces in India and Overseas, his specialization is naturally in the area of Sales Training (All levels with Presentation, Negotiation, Key/ Strategic Accounts Management & Managerial Skills for all sectors), Bid Proposal/ Capture Planning/ Management Trainings, Retail Sales, Customer Service & Customer Retention Programs, Training for Prevention & Collection of Debt, Self & Personal Development Programs (Time Management, Teamwork & Team Building, Business Etiquette & Personal Grooming, Leadership & Managerial Skills, People Management Skills, Train-the-Trainer etc), including preparation of Custom-designed Business Manuals for Internal (HR, Induction, and Sales etc) & External use (Instruction, User Manuals).

Gerard has successfully conducted over 5500 Trainings & Workshops all across India, Middle East, Africa, Europe & S.E. Asia. Besides public programs conducted regularly, both in India & Overseas, he has some of the top names as clients whom he services from Single Owners to large Public & Government undertakings, covering all sectors, for their in-house needs.

His website: www.CollectionSkills.com is the only one in this part of the world to be featured in the 'Collections & Credit Risk Magazine-USA' under 'Who's Who in Training'. Gerard is author of 23 books (as on April 2021),

A few of the secular books being:

1. Bite-sized Bits on Commonsense Management
2. Heart to Heart on Life's Principles'
3. How to become a Successful Manager
4. The Sales Professionals' Master Workbook of S.Y.S.T.E.M.S
5. The Professional Business Email Etiquette Handbook & Guide
6. The Professional Business Video-Conferencing Etiquette Handbook & Guide
7. Professional Presentation Skills
8. Exceptional Customer Service

…And some of his most recent Christian Books being:

1. 'A Bouquet of Praises for My KING',
2. Christian Jokes for the Serious Religious' Folks!
3. Jesus Healed You!
4. Praise24Ever!
5. The 5G Network of GOD
6. Building Faith over F.E.A.R-FACE EVERYTHING AND RISE with JESUS
7. Hebrew and Greek Praise and Worship Words
8. Godly Mothers' and Grandmothers' Bible Story time for Kids
9. Miracles of JESUS in Pictures
10. Raise your Praise All 365 Days: (SON Rise Praises from Genesis to Revelation to begin each day!)
11. Thanking GOD with an Attitude of Gratitude
12. Meditating on the Attributes of GOD
13. Puppet Scripts

Besides regularly contributing to business & trade journals, including international ones such as the 'Creative Training Techniques' and the 'Sales News' of the U.S.A, He is also a member of several prestigious bodies & trade associations, having participated in many Conferences & Workshops in India & Overseas.

Prior to his last assignment of leading &managing a large MNC as head, Gerard had a 3-year stint in the Middle East as a Consultant with a leading British Consultancy Firm. As the past 'Official Country Representative' for the International Business Award- 'THE STEVIES'-(the business world's own Oscar) for about 4 years- he ensured a few Indian companies that qualify for the same every year!

Gerard can be contacted at:
E: mail: training@Sales-Training.in
training@CollectionSkills.com

Websites:

www.Sales-Training.in
www.EtiquetteWorks.in
www.CollectionSkills.com
www.RetailSalesTraining.in
www.SalesTrainingIndia.com
www.ManualPreparation.com
www.TrainingWithPuppets.com
www.FirstContactAcademy.com
www.Skills2Win-Just4Teens.com
www.SalesAndMarketingRecruiter.com

www.ingramcontent.com/pod-product-compliance
Lightning Source LLC
LaVergne TN
LVHW041224200726
843507LV00013B/2569